Songs From a Schizophrenic

Liam Zevoughn

SONGS FROM A SCHIZOPHRENIC

Liam Zevoughn

XULON PRESS

Xulon Press
2301 Lucien Way #415
Maitland, FL 32751
407.339.4217
www.xulonpress.com

Unless otherwise indicated, Scripture quotations taken from the King James Version (KJV) – *public domain.*

Paperback ISBN-13: 978-1-6628-2623-8
Hard Cover ISBN-13: 978-1-6628-2624-5
Ebook ISBN-13: 978-1-6628-2625-2

Hello, my name is Liam Zevoughn Daniel Dishner. This book is a reason I'm still alive. When I was 13 I suffered immensely. A terrible thing happened to me & i am so grateful to be alive still. It is a miracle from God, no doubt.

In April of 2017, I started suffering a psychotic episode. During this episode I suffered the strongest delusions & hallucinations I've ever experienced. I believed I was an "art savior". I believed people would pray to me to bless their art. This simply cannot be for i am not sinless. I believed with all my heart that I was 2Pac's prophecy. I still think I am his prophecy sometimes. I believed he was alive for a long time but part of me says he could not have stayed quiet this long. Part of me says he hasn't stayed quiet. I don't know what 2Pac prayed for & I don't know with certainty that he is alive but I believed I was his prayers come to life. I don't know how he would stay so quiet for so long. I was terrified every second of everyday. I thought that when I was 13 & died numerous times that I had died for art so none of it would have to go to Hell. I thought aliens were constantly watching me. I felt their presence. I thought they did things to my body while I slept. I thought the government was after me. I thought the FBI was after me. I suffered many other delusions.

What you must first understand is I would never make anything like this up. Even before I got hurt I would have never entertained the idea of making anything like this up.

In April of 2017, I was praying constantly. I don't know how long I prayed but it must have been weeks & weeks. Well one night while I was praying in my parked car, Jesus Christ spoke to me while listening to Brand New & put my entire body at one of the gates of heaven. As he spoke I felt a cloud of resurrection fill my entire body, very slowly. That's the best I can describe it. The best way I can describe the gates is hand-carved by angels. Absolutely flawless. Golden gates with so many intricate pearl designs with giant purple amethyst rocks protruding from the gate. It was like I got the welcome I didn't get when I was 13. This moment pushed me into unprecedented psychosis & I'm so glad that it did.

Every vein of my body was filled with an everlasting peace which is indescribable. I truly felt what it is like to be in heaven. I cried. I can say with confidence nothing on earth is worth missing heaven for. This is the highlight of my very existence. On a different occasion i also heard God's voice. It sounded like flowing water, like a river or stream. At the same time i understood exactly what He was saying. On a separate occasion I heard an angel speak to me. I also had a dream, likely in April of 2017, that I astral traveled into hell. Once I arrived Jesus took these white cloth coverings off my eyes & I saw what I believed to be Satan standing there with a giant ball of light in his hands. I don't know if I blinked or what happened but it just registered as a music note to me. It looked like it wasn't being taken care of. It looked like a rusty music note. I've had numerous dreams about hell since this occurred.

My episode lasted until March of 2018. These writings in the first part of this book were written during my episode, that's why they don't have dates on them. A lot of times I think time is an illusion.

God changed my entire life. I wrote very differently in the past compared to now. I'm saying now that I'm not above writing fiction. Fiction can be beautiful. I started writing at 13

Hello,

This book is a product of mental illness & passion. These writings are my whole life. I love every second of my writing time. Never dull. I think this is a big reason I'm still alive.

In this book you will find emotions which are raw & uncut.

I must say that my biggest inspiration is 2Pac. I wish I could thank him for showing me how ardent a human being can become. Beyond 2Pac i give most credit to God. Who has loved me uncon-ditionally & provided me with the gifts to write as I do. I would be absolutely nothing without him. God changed my everything in one night. In less than thirty seconds. I prayed that God would give me a career with music ever since i can remember & this book is just like a piece of music. 2Pac said you can a cappella rap. So that's what I've been trying to do ever since i was wee little. Typically, if it's not about music, or like music, or somehow related to an artist i just don't care about it. I listen to music con-stantly every day. I cannot get enough. I have always been this way, my whole life. I cannot recall a time i wasn't thinking about or listening to music.

CASTED CROWN

Isolation
& fear have
Cast a crown
Upon my flesh
I live in the past
I ask why God tied a noose around my neck
Had I lived too fast?
Had my ambition been next to zero
Had I risen past my mission to become a hero
My casted crown
Comforts
But does not progress
I am falling down to hurt
Pain
With pain I do obsess
Some bleed for
Life
I bleed for arrest
Some bleed for love
I bleed for the rest & lack thereof
To love
Is pain wasted
I live in a world
Where most inside become the tainted
Liam Zevoughn

EVERYTHING

The Lord sent me an angel
Her eyes I still see today
To this I cling
Within them I could see everything
For a glimpse in time
I could see life without despair
Your eyes
Told me I wasn't even there
This is true
I
Love
You
The tide may rise enough to strangle
I love you
Angel
Liam Zevoughn

I CALL

I am among the breathless
Among words said
I am dead
Still I be young & restless
Ill to see
We sung & tested
Waters
Still I be dumb & fretless for I could never love a daughter
Lavender, O, I call
Bring me sweet arrest
Laughter be small so sing in my sheets
Lest
There be another
Test me
Lover
At length; for I haven't the strength to be alone in covers
This, my ode to you
Shall be forever
Rinse by cold waters
She's my only hope to never die; I cry to thee almighty's daughter
I love you for He is your father
Liam Zevoughn

HELL

You will rise
In time; in fate
Perform a mocking wry because some try to intimidate
Just heal
Hate has no place
But that love be so real

All my friends say the same
All my friends days are not
Without pain
They say hell is hot
Today they want to pray for rain
& relieve grey body rot

All hail she
Miss endeavored beauty
Tell to me
Means of a heavy duty
Thou art a luminescence
Perfect are thee
Entomb me in essence
Sweet lavender tree
Liam Zevoughn

STOIC

Why
Sung I
Lungs full of asphalt
& led
I flew by the orchard & stalled
I recall being among the dead
Poetic obligation
My words are all said
Heroic declaration
Am I supposed to land?
Was this a test
Maybe if I get close enough death will tell who I am
I feel no pain
No shame
I, modern stoic, earned a name
Over this broken vessel
I cried & dreamed
My flaws I will lessen
I died but screamed lament on site
God, I have questions
Why do people dislike me
I am dead just to spite me
I can't get past what my life might be
Liam Zevoughn

ARTERY

Some move past it
Some lock it away in a cage
Life is joy?
This boy is in traffic because he cannot move past his rage
Transfixed
Obsessive
Who could lift a preadolescence depression?
Auburn nimbus encased a will
So dire
The boy's heart throbbed until he surrendered to fire
One of the most coy he sobbed & killed his ember
Another life did he desire
To do this he ended his own
Must passionate die young & alone
Has every good-hearted hung their bones
Hardly
Long live this artery the hood started among their homes
I, stoic, will call you encouragement in sung tones
Who started me?
You are never alone
Long live this artery
Liam Zevoughn

ORCHIDS

I will be inspired in the garden
Enchantment
A small fire somewhere is alive
Beside all wired lights there is life
An atmosphere of throbbing pulses
None to fear
Audible whispered voices
Please take me here
Be there peace where humanity departed
Little orchids
Eat remains
Blood dripping organism
Nature does forbid
Mortal veins
Hail this cycle in our prison
Crawl even lighter
Just to survive
A small fire somewhere is alive
Liam Zevoughn

Dust & Leaves

So much easier to breathe
Up with the clouds
Lighter & free
I found myself empty
Never safe, never sound
Breathe
Clouds
Free
See I never found something so empty
Reason
Be
The dead shall prevail thee
Unwelcome ghost
Find the trap which ensnares me
You'll have what lusts the most
Speaking to a mortal mind was pleasure
Dust & leaves
I seek the normal kind; I am treasure
Recipe of greed
Even my own was pure
Liam Zevoughn

Hope Floats

A cold September morning
I recall your hope
Breathe for me
A cold September morning
Frozen rain caused me pain
Misery too; I love you but what have you done to your brain?
You're broke but don't choke
I recall hope floats
This morning you are finally free
Today you see now breathe for me
I have wept
Your bones must have bent
Today you have slept & wondered why
I cry for you were crushed in lament
Don't wonder too high
So you thought you'd hang a rope
You thought never to satisfy desire
Thought you already died so this ain't dire
Liam Zevoughn

Heart

If I fall asleep without you
Forget my existence
Benefit from the doubt
That I'm breathing
& continue
Beating
Life to me would be no more
I would decompose too
Everything I know will part
I could not live without you
My only heart
Liam Zevoughn

Blood Clots

Inside me bleeds the hue of red
At times such as these I see I am naught
At times I think I am dead
Oh my, the potency of my thoughts
What thread would quicken the feeling of distraught
The ceiling confines me as I rot
Floods of my tears hold back; all life is naught
Blood clots hurting me again to the black I have lost but fought
In my prison I bleed
What more can come of pain but rot
When my heart beats no more read my clots and see life stole the
potency of my thoughts
Liam Zevoughn

GRIM

My lungs feel so heavy
Insane
The pen be so vain but I died for this pain already
Took me awhile
But if I could go back to that photo I would smile
Will I remember her name when I visit her in Hell
Call me stoic
I thought the most poetic I could do was killing myself
During one episode I could see
Understand
Death would not take me
The plan
Underrates me
My past cuts but I wonder the fates that await me
So please stand
A flock of tidings surrounded him
But I am so uninviting
Call that grim
I sometimes think about how words have rooted me
To this place
I know that death has eluded me
If there is a piece that doesn't belong it's my face
I am in awe of the devils influence and might
In a dark cave we went with sight
Me & the Lord were the only light
We were there for all the night
& in my mind
I saw true pleasure
A gift of infectious blight
The Lord had blessed me with the right treasure
& the cave was so empty and tight
& engraved in the side were people
Never
Never had I witnessed such evil

But as if to cradle a baby
A big goat
Stood out & lulled to me a rusty music note
Liam Zevoughn

OKAY

My body is on fire
Yet my mind is soft
I search for the faulty wire
That makes me lost
My name is wrong
Call me homeless
Say you won't be long
Find your mind & roam this
This is my song
I love an eternity
We shall thrive
We shall burn infernally & miss deprived
I am okay
I am alive
Sometimes things you say make me die inside
You are your own
Tangent, soft, loving
My lament gets lost in a trusting lavender well
Soothe my bones & release me from a shell
I love this place
I love things you say
It is you I desire
I will be okay
Liam Zevoughn

SWEET SURRENDER

Thou art only maybes
There are sweet surrenders
We are but desperate navies
The crow can't remember
The dead he plucked an eye from
My eye can see
My eye is free but on the run
Under the bright sun
Famine be plenty
Assailants & crack addicts
The poor be many
But this I remember
Don't tell any
There are sweet surrenders
The bird which flies
Grew a down
Lost an eye
He flew around & crossed the sky
He lewd the crown & tossed it aside
The down shoed a sound & found the tide
A love
A purpose was inside
A trust
A church service
Confide
Confess
Love the guy that died for your purpose
One day the bird burned in an ember
He could not cheat
We found a sweet surrender
One harmless defeat
Liam Zevoughn

STREAM

Does your God make dreams?
Drink from an eternal river
My God makes streams
We do love his deeds, us, the sinners
I live in laughter
An ever after
Forgive a life of disaster
Forgive me & nail me to plywood but please
Love me lavender
God gave me a dream
& still I fall
Like a drug fiend all I do is call & he fails to answer
I am so small but give me a chance or
Love the rest
Bestow me a dance or hellish arrest
I ate your cancer
Now all you are is free
I am the angel in your stream
Why won't he answer me?
Have I left my dream?
Liam Zevoughn

SPIDER

I love you art
A sweet song to thee
I want to rip my skull apart
An endeavor I hope you see
& still my white flag ebbs
Cool in the breeze
My will & I are caught in a spiders web
Dear death
Please don't tease
I must say, the poverty stings
Nothing more painful than listening to a dead man sing
With this pain I deal
Down this road is real
Yet it is around the woe I feel
My only friend is fear so
I can't be your hero
My flag ebbs
But I am caught in a web
Get away? How can I start?
One, two, three
I love you art
A sweet song to thee
So much struggling
I cannot remember
I bestow to you a sweet surrender
O, what an exquisite web
How I long to pine beside her
If I could only find my bed
Thank you spider
No chance for a treaty
So eat me
Liam Zevoughn

FAULT

This foreign pen
Writes in blood
That's how much love I'm in
You have been lying
To cover something
I have been dying
For
Your sweet nothing
Baby-fake madonna
I sometimes forget your existence
Call me dead
Nirvana
Cleanse your wounds & I will rinse it
With salt
In the dark
You have earned a fault
I churn
I will fill your heart with salt
You will feel my burn
Boil over & surrender
Liam Zevoughn

SCARED

Consciousness
Blades of grass faired
In this square
Help me because I am scared
Consciousness
Drive-bys exist
Watch this
Follow the bullets
Words of ardent wisdom I cannot resist
White rice
Courtney Ray
If my words suffice
Your life lays in soil bays
Liam Zevoughn

METTLE

Here I sit transfixed with oblivion
My heart longs for mettle
Could redemption settle a sway?
Could God do what he wanted with me?
Could he do that anyway?
Have I lived forever against a mortal's test?
Haven't I lived enough today?
This why life has death
But Immortality was the goal
My heart longs for mettle
Upon a poet
Beseeched a vice
Upon arrival of the west
A piece of himself died
Liam Zevoughn

THE LOST

I have
Broke in
Too many homes
& murdered
A nostalgic, warm
Medicine
Curse my withered
Worn
Skeleton
I will
I can
At all costs
I withstand cold
I am not the mold but God panned the lost
As if I hold the season
Captive
How do I
Live?
I take
But never give
Liam Zevoughn

ANGEL

I
Am of
Sin
Without a sword
I will crawl out of my skin
Please be with me Lord
My own will
Dangles
& ill are thee
Entangled
Twisted though they are
Blistered, as my heart
I will be their angel
They have snuffed
Each other
This is true
But enough has come & I will suffer for you
All seats in my house are pews
Come unto
Forgiveness
Live & witness I will suffer for you
I will search and eat your sickness
No more hurt for you or your kin
I will crawl out of my skin
To mend a pain you live in
I will bleed dry this prison
To muster anew
For me, love only strangles
Let me be your angel
Let me be your angel
Let me be your angel
Let me be your angel
Let me be your angel
I hurt

Apostasy I have witnessed
I will search & eat your sickness
Liam Zevoughn

BETTER

How wrong must last
Please depart
I have been sad forever
Long live my car crash heart
Will anything get better?
Liam Zevoughn

SEW

When will they see
When will they know
Your heart is a vacancy
Which music sews

After death I write
I was a certain way in life
But through love & faith
I was changed by Jesus Christ
Liam Zevoughn

DEAR TITAN

Star dust & sin
Here I am
Only dim
We are far
Still your life begins
Mold for me
Methane symphonies
Be it a cold sore
Not to witness
Your moons carry this
Infection
Brother Enceladus has affection
I find only car rust & binge
Dear Titan
Star dust & sin
Here I am
Only so dim
Liam Zevoughn

PRETEND

Timeless enclosure
Celestial, cold frame
To this I have exposure
Potential one cannot tame
I will ponder into your hardened eye
Without being ashamed
I will wonder into your garden & not know why
This has not been a golden fame
I will scathe the dirt with a heavy sigh
Feeling among friends
I will bathe in the earth & look to the sky
Just to pretend
I wonder why I am crying
I cannot mend
My heart; we are dying
Every person appears smart
To my inner eye we are not apart
Could I be lying?
We are but gracious art
We are only dying
Liam Zevoughn

CORPSE

Another anguishing pain
Of course
I know not why it hurts for I am only a corpse
So vain
Another night; I am drained
My life, my soul, my brain
A wife, a goal, my veins
So completely vain
Hot tar shall stain
My insides
Of course
I used to love to watch the tides but I am only a corpse
I don't feel the rain
Bury me, please, depart
I hurt my head
I said my heart stopped so long ago I can't remember how to start
I am dead
Liam Zevoughn

I Feel You

I knew you were there
Lingering
Holding to life
You too have this flare
Tingling, molding, right
Judgement, accusation, so called influenced strife
This is what they do
Could cut the judgment with a knife
Just know that
I feel you
Liam Zevoughn

WHITE IVORY VINE

I am the white thriving ivory vine
Breathe but hark this
I am free
I am free but be in darkness
Broken
I am so
All my friends have spoken but died so long ago
God bless the seed which sings
Hark this, but breathe
I am in darkness, see, but try to use broken things
I have lost but sustained
I constantly remember the price is pain
Remember what growth brings?
Will I ever stop trying to use these broken things?
I am alone
God bless the seed which sings
Men lost their minds
Bless again the men who kept their own
I am the white thriving ivory vine that binds
God bless the seed which sings alone
Liam Zevoughn

LESSEN

Long live my friend
I will ascend
Again
Though this cure be pure
God will punish this pen
Ink from this quill
Has killed again
Murdered the will to depend
These pieces make the thesis of God will punish this pen
I dwindle on the rope
See me choke
If only I could hold to this little hope
See
My nostalgic revelry
Shall be forever
I could choke on hope
Could you pull my lever
To answer your question of more praise
I will never again lessen
Lest it be a flag of war you raise
Liam Zevoughn

Plume

I won't ever let you down
Excuse, excuse
I won't ever let you drown
Muse abuse
O, the garden is in bloom
A mild, electric fuse heavy as plume
A sappy, tender sound
There is a small child growing in your womb
I hope you are happy now
Liam Zevoughn

Anew

Punish me for the kids
Disdain this pen
No pain again; score for orchids

Love to death
Keep breathing
Alas, this depth has wrought hurting feelings

Brand me as New
Inspiration
Until we meet again, Joel, you have justification
Liam Zevoughn

NEVER MIND

I am dry clay
Dear grapevine
I want to die today
Never mind
Liam Zevoughn

Moons

My cold heart
Oh no, I'm smart
Amid blood moons
Grows my cancer
Dear Alice; avid mushroom
In mystery, in death lies the answer
What to do
I love art
Who are you?
I've got a cold heart
I am blue
Oh no, I'm smart
Liam Zevoughn

Younger Days

I went to school
I made a friend, a bird
I'm just a tool
He made it; I've been absurd
Ignore this too
I'm a liar
Today, I must say
I miss you Tyler
I recall the lament endured
Woe tis:
Of all pence I'm sure
Where is Joseph?
Hunger today
Persuasion?
I recall the conversation of our younger day
Liam Zevoughn

MYSTERY

Awake in shock
Yellow sock
Mystery
I had a dream with 2Pac
Hello clock
You're history
Welcoming church
Evil lurks
Hello thoughts of misery
God works
No more hurt
Yellow socks mean mystery
Liam Zevoughn

Consciousness

Blades of grass faired
In this square
Help me because I am scared
Consciousness
Drive bys exist
Watch this:
Follow the bullets
Words of ardent wisdom I cannot resist
White rice
Courtney Ray
If my words suffice
Your life lays in soil bays
Liam Zevoughn

BLESSINGS

O, cold heart
Count your blessings
Or so depart
I cannot posses music sessions
Long down unpaved roads
Artists learned lessons
I own the graved, sewn question
Hell is hot
Cold heart
Tell not your scars
Time to start
Hell rots but not far
Liam Zevoughn

Feel Me?

My beloved grapevine
How I have missed you
Beloved sunshine
Laud to interest; which hath kissed
Blue
What is wrong with me
I remember the day
We sung a song to thee
I surrendered pain
Please take it away
Affection
I never knew you
Rejection
I recall too
Dear anguish, I sung a song to thee
What is wrong with me
Grapevine
Please deal me
I'm fine
Feel me?
Liam Zevoughn

A Union

It
Is
A Crime
To take someone
So high
Then leave
I speak in rhyme
They become restless &
Unhappy
The lavender tree
Will never forgive you
She's catatonic & hurting
She will never forgive you
In a dark wood
A union grew forlorn
Their hearts are torn
God, be with them
It is you I warn
I speak in rhyme
She will never forgive
A union grew forlorn
It is you I warn
Liam Zevoughn

Halo

But you look like a white light to me

You saved me

But why

You saved me

But I
(I love this particular bag of bones)
(I pour salt in all my wounds)
(God be gracious, in separate places)
(I just want to be your angel)
(Is it okay to fall in love with the flesh?)
(Killed my lamb) relate to Jesus

I'm fitted for my halo
The best objects have come free
Something inside me is burning
A fascist subtlety

Show this baby some love & be saved
I have killed so many pieces of myself
Still I carry dead parts
Liam Zevoughn

FATE

Dear white light
Fate
I am starlight & wine
Here I fight this state
Forever I shall stay divine
Liam Zevoughn

Seven Tides

Itty bitty wrongs
God help he loves all our pretty songs
Outside flings a fawn
He confides by singing along
Heaven in his dreams
See flies
He cries, he knows not what it means
Seven tides
Brought feeling to tear his seams
Petrified
On his brother in heaven he leans
Testified
Of other leavened dreams
He sung a song & died
But his love only multiplied
One itty bitty song
His entire life
Was pretty wrong
Forever kind
He won't be long but
Never mind
Liam Zevoughn

THRESH

Searching for warmth
Yellow socks mean mystery
Hurting in swarms
Hello thoughts which comfort me
I am torn
To love history
More than flesh
To this I am sworn
Mortal thresh to see
Swarms
Normal, fresh, empty
Secrets I have told
Hurting in swarms
I am so cold & searching for warmth
Hello cots which seen history
Yellow socks mean mystery
Thorns insert meaning
I am screaming & hurting in swarms
Help me I'm screaming
I am torn
Tossed normal flesh
Crossed the mortal thresh
I am sworn
Liam Zevoughn

HEAVY

I kill
Heavy pill
Consciousness, I confess
Vain
I write this in distress
Which pain dost thou detest?
Insane
This way I am best
Blood stain
Veins long for rest
Derogatory shrill
Do not test
Heavy pill
I kill
Which pain dost thou detest?
Liam Zevoughn

Avid Mushroom

We breathe bacteria
Breed hysteria
Among the dead
You know
We grow
Amid blood moons
In your dreams
We scream
We are Avid Mushrooms
Liam Zevoughn

SEA SHELL

I listened to the sea shell
Learning well
So, I want to know can you paint a picture of a burning Hell

Ms. Jane can only please us
Can you fathom the living Jesus

I listened to the sea shell
Learning well
So, I want to know can you paint a picture of a burning Hell
Liam Zevoughn

INCOMPETENCE

Incompetence
What a great place to hide
I want to write
Says my sick insides
This life although seems rougher
Alone
I sank in suffer
Have I earned my own?
Time to hide; this
Says my sick insides

I am sad to be
Once again a mirror I flee
God I do not like what I see
Sickening lore
A creature
beat upon my door
Not to be
It said all this is yours
If you bow and worship me
Liam Zevoughn

JESSE'S CLASS

Don't have enough strength
For a messy task
But surely as a cure
I remember falling asleep in Jesse's class
Long live the pure &
The spiritual grass
May the deep outlast
This time I will ask for the fast to be counted last
My sanity & I will dash
An evanescent
No time to crash or lure
I remember falling asleep surely as a cure
No questions, no lessons
This pen does not deter
Confessing
Obsessing
Listen to her

Hatin'
Will not suffice
But Kaitlyn I will not be the one to roll the dice
Obscene
Transgression
Dear nicotine, with you I have obsession
Listen to me pur
No lesson
Surely as a cure I will drown any question
Purely for her, I will strangle
Just messin'
I had love enough, this was rough, you were the fallen angel
I am what you call a sir
Surely
As
A

Cure
Liam Zevoughn

BRUISE

Sickness had me
Suns & moons
For once I'd like to see Jesus be happy & become a perfume

Sickness had me
A hematoma will lose
No one said this so badly
No one told you that this was a bruise
Liam Zevoughn

Warmth of the Sun

& was this a test?
Unworthy
I will search & cleanse the window of quest
& you won't hurt me
I'll just go then
To the angle
The chairs are heavy so you don't throw them
Discerning & burning as an angel

May God heal the spite
The war
I am in a psych ward with many vices to fight for & taking my
own medicine but Lord could I have some cure for my skeleton?
He can't help he was born of the scum
Can't breathe
Can't believe you can't take away the warmth of the sun
Consult with the trees
Looking for something fair in in binges
Syringes
Hinges will not hold
On the meniscus of fringes with a cardinal on the marigold

Let us praise God for swarms of fun
Let us be done
The warmth of the sun
Frees
But never confines
Bring forth
The sweet lavender of fine
Taste
& with elegance in place I will taste a sweet pace but say it took
all of 30 minutes to fall from grace
Distaste
Shall not stain

No lace
No sorrow
I will erase
The arguments of tomorrow

Such a dove
Will suffice
Much love, much love, much love
White rice

More than this I will become
A mess
God bless the warmth of the sun
Liam Zevoughn

BEAM

My creed's song
After awhile some friends are family
After eons
Your rival left you to insanity
Pacing
Tracing
Erasing will not suffice
Facing a hell raiser among mice–I will roll the dice

Agápi to the one
Who feels
Agápi to the sun
The only real
I will peel
& contract the appropriate zeal
Every instinct to feel
Undeniably is buying me a ticket to something that is real

I will not be greeted
I fall with a thud
Tell me how it feels to be defeated by the shedding of blood
I will not be greeted
But notice the life of moss
Tell me how it feels to be defeated by a cross

Though my position fenced me
-I mean-
-I dreamed-
You will not be against me
I need a beam
Liam Zevoughn

ARMISTICE

May it intervene
Be found
It seems the only sound
Is peace
May fire cease
May your casted crown
Be released

This is my first time on the meniscus
Of shore
I will stay & rinse this
Gorgeous war
No doubt the sun shines on existence but I just can't do this anymore

May this scream perfection
Intervene
Quiet time is mine for reflection & forget the obscene
Forget the sewn
Forget the bullets I had blown, I'm finally going home

& the truancy I will miss
Let's save the grave for another day
Sheer brilliance- armistice- youth
Forever I will be drawn to the truth
Liam Zevoughn

Part Two

Abstract

One time I sink fitting in frames
Every cop I ever spit on is locking their chains
Searching for meaning
How could this be sane when they want to kill me while
I'm dreaming?
& what of fame?
& what of finches?
Again, now & then, I am plastered to a canvas inches below the blood
Hinges
Will not hold, i am constantly searching for bud
I cry like vapor
Get by with veins
Every canvas or paper plane is made never in vain for I am there
to bless the gain
One day I slid out of the frame
& I splattered on the ground
I found a world broken by lust
I was not flattered but wound
Down a swirl I spoke in dust
Calling, calling, calling
Breath of the sprawling, I awoke in cuffs
Falling
The best frame I ever fit in was that of peace
So you must keep drawing
When will this lust turn to vapor? Cease?
I am just calling but all I find is paper
Have I yet earned favor in this crease?
I will grow, Lord knows, but how could I be an art savior in peace?
Liam Zevoughn 11/29/19

GARY'S IDOL

I watched your idol fall
In its place you chose a Christmas tree
I unlocked your chain & ball
It's not a race but He rose past riches & royalty
Under this pressure I dull & stall
Such a blunder-your idol hadn't a chance to crawl
Into His graces
No wonder you cough
You pull but pranced around it all when it came to celestial faces
& the null can only crawl
I could never mind the pitches you tee
I watched your idol fall
In its place you chose a Christmas tree
Liam Zevoughn 12/21/19

PETRIFIED

I am aching, manic in my home
Petrified
I cannot deny the panic in my bones
I rectified
Sung tones
But how
Can I communicate
The distress of my mind
Now
I can best describe my lifeline
As she
Taking and banding it with tones
So yes, I am aching, manic in my home
I cannot deny the panic in my bones
Liam Zevoughn 2/4/20

MOCKING BIRD

The mocking bird is calling me a liar
This quill will kill again
Hail the shocking word that began my fire
May it fill your head
Rail the flocking verbs that can inspire
& find me there
My lips stung with truth
Confined & scared
This ship has sunk the youth
Nothing is fair
I am spared
Leave this note alone but wired
The rocking hurts but I'm falling inspired
The mocking bird is calling me a liar
Liam Zevoughn 12/7/19

CATHEDRALS

I wish I could write what screams in cathedrals
Rinse away what autumn's needles wrought
Since I am at the bottom
I am starting to rot
& what of fame?
I am only a convalescent
That one girl; cathedrals scream your name
And I, having lessened, am shamed
I bequeath
An ever after
Numbs me dumb but I leave to you a sheer light of laughter
Us orphans are fostered
Sticks & tin may break the skin but
We're all in & rostered
Rejoice with voice the lamb was slaughtered
Choice was the love which, before us, fathered
I miss the good, righteous dreams I had under that needle
I wish I could write what screams in cathedrals
Liam Zevoughn 11/21/19

DREAM OF YOU

I'd rather dream of you than nothing at all
Liam Zevoughn 12/3/20

JIMMY

Can't give fright without terror
Fallow zones
Can't live life without the light bearer
& birds with their hallow bones

God bless the back sanctuary
Odd confess their sins and tip me
Bless my dawg jimmy and his immaculate vocabulary

Find the vine to grow to
& this will prosper
The Lord keeps telling me He knows you
Find the time and foster

I'd open if you would leave
The past
Pray for my uncle Timmy
In sung tones
The Lord is with us Jimmy
& birds with their hallow bones

A fallow tree phones
To the underground
& birds with their hallow bones
Jimmy, you are found

No doubt the bird has it
Musical bones
I heard you dropped some acid
Now look how you've grown
Liam Zevoughn 8/3/19

Shrill tides

To feel is to sing
& to respect is to care
But how can I sit there and ask myself anything?
I loved the truth & desired to dare

& in autumn's shrill tides
I found a vacancy
My ill eyes grew a dull hue
I found a purposeful latency that became you

In autumn's shrill tides
The bottom of the leaf piles became my home
Rotten am I
Forgotten for awhile but now I see I am not alone

This is the
Gospel of my heart
Thank you Alyssa, for doing the impossible
Today I will again start
Liam Zevoughn 8/31/19

I DREAMED

I dreamed first
I had an unconscious thirst
I dreamed of cataclysmic dirt I even dreamed of an elephant
giving birth

I dreamed I sailed
My mind on fire flailed in the breeze
A fiend failed to be but I called on God with cordial ease

I dreamed I got high
A nirvana bemused me
Marijuana I craved loosely and then I died

I dreamed I was wondering in the night
I found vacancy in a fallow tree
I dreamed of a taken sea that crashed into a black beach; what a sight

Let this song give a new birth
Long live my unconscious thirst
Liam Zevoughn 9/17/19

MICHELLE

On the day I entered your kingdom, Lord
There were no tears
Elatedness & joy in sheer
On the day I entered your kingdom
I had not fear
I was found by
Grace
I've been around enough to know
This place
I've been down the rough & still sew
It's not a race
What I have to tell
Will bring you passion
I will be true to Hell
Like a sea I have yet to fathom
Truth is I miss you, Michelle
I hope to bring you cheer
Ring some bell
Your kingdom
I desire more than
Hell
But Michelle, will you sing some spell?
Sing some
Spell
On the day I entered your kingdom I hadn't another thought of Hell
Liam Zevoughn 10/11/19

YARN

I never meant to cause you harm
Please depart
I am made of yarn
I can see right through your poised heart
Amongst your voodoo enriched toys
In the noise within the dark
You found me
Heed a butterfly's kiss
Read my lips
I know that you are yearning for me
But please stop
Stop burning me
I never meant to cause you harm
Would someone darn?
So I am made of yarn
Now I see the one yearning is me
So please stop
Stop burning me
Liam Zevoughn 6/1/19

AILMENT

A broken ailment
Rendered you to surrender
So you may; it's okay
To rest on the seventh day
I will plant a hypnotic tree in your honor
Is this wrong or
Pleasant
My sins ring in the ear of every confessant
May the planets align
& may they remember
My name
I speak in rhyme
One surrenders never in vain
I will redefine
I will inspire this time
The growth of your tree has rendered me omniscient
I shall grace the leaves of thyme with my song
Though my song isn't
Pure
I will lessen your sorrow for your sake
I will create a cure & tomorrow I will forsake
Desperation
This tree will be all knowing too
The dead shall prevail thee
The free will all be sewing their hearts due
To the sin which weighs
Where to begin when
The rest of the day
Is shrouded
What to say when
The mind is clouded
We relish in sun rays
We take a turn & see
So I will not say "I can't"

I will plant a hypnotic tree
Liam Zevoughn 5/26/19

UNCONVENTIONAL

I should have burned you when I had the chance
Have I yet earned a dance?
If you die in torrents
Every spider in the forest shall lament with gracious architecture
Unconventional
Forever sighing formants sent to confess for
The odds
May these words never destroy
May they please the gods
May they inspire the jovial boy without facades
I churned but got sad in advance
Unconventional
I should have burned you when I had the chance
This writing was pleasure; intentional finesse
You are treasure
Never settle for less
Liam Zevoughn 5/26/19

SUFFER

I remember
Being in the pain
I would have lit my way
If not for the snuffer
So vain
An angel sent me there to suffer
Liam Zevoughn 4/16/19

TIDES

I fled from the lies for her heart was faded
I seen the celestial
Purple rocks with gold & grated
We are the tides
But I'm back, reincarnated
Are stars really lies?

She was dead inside but I think we dated
She died is what I said in slight
Yet her frame not mutilated
How could one shine so bright from afar
How could one give such light
& not be a dead star?
Liam Zevoughn 4/16/19

RELIEF

Grief
What an old state
I'm breaking all my teeth
Goodbye to you, my dear soulmate
Hell is hot
Hell is dark
So my friends say
Make due with what you've got
Because we all have to pay
Relief
What an odd feeling
Certainly supernatural
Is this belief enough to prove God's being?
Is this faux?
Long live perfection
& it's sad truth
Long live the fire's perplextion
If we only knew
Liam Zevoughn 4/19/19

MY KINGDOM

My eyes do advert
Since you have burned
It took time to learn my kingdom is not of this earth
Now an urn you have earned
& my sanity has fled
God, bless the paranoid
I am seeing red
These days
O, to live as a void; look away
Could God do what he wanted? Could he anyway?
I am not a flower from this dirt
Not conceit
So my kingdom grows not of this earth
Long live the rose from concrete
Harmless defeat
These feelings I do assert
For this immortal piece shall not churn
But since you have burned my eyes do advert
Wrong lasts no more & will part
My kingdom is not of this earth
Long live my car crash heart
Liam Zevoughn 4/19/19

SLEEP

In depths of paranoia
I await thee
In the
Void

& In my mind
Screams a latency unknown
What might become
What must devise
Is you
What godly dust can despise such a dreamlike blue?

& you are my stronghold
Fortified & timeless
Fold my mind
Grab hold of my line
Because I am throwing it

So I await thee in the void
Scream my name
I dream the same as a boy
& just as deep
Haunt me & leave a dream
Dear sleep
Liam Zevoughn 9/7/19

PALACE

My blood is still thickening
I bathe in red
I am so ill
It is sickening
My skin does harden
Call me callous
Once upon a time I grew in a garden
In a sunlit palace
& the dirt which I knew sang a song
"You can do anything; you're never wrong."
This departure killed me inside
& the sun which I knew had grown malice
It is growth which I dream of
& this garden; this palace
Was called love
Liam Zevoughn 4/20/19

Spider's Web

I am not dead
Just maybe, won't someone save me
I am caught in a spider's web
A deadly dream
Shaky & bemused by a web-like seam
At any cost
Take me confused as a fiend
I am lost
I find myself dreaming I was part of a team
I was tossed
& now the dark architecture has entangled me
I am so tired
How has my own heart angled me?
I wanted to inspire
Now I find I am wired
As in a dream
Listen to the words I said
For now just leave me be
I think I am dead
Caught in a spider's web
Liam Zevoughn 4/22/19

WOUND

Room
I am attuned
But torn by a fresh wound
We praise those who have much to say
In the void, I am praying
You're screaming but I don't know what you're saying
Please scream anyway
I died on moms anniversary
Seen me gasp for air
I hardly consider death an adversary
I could breathe at the Ferris wheel fair
I am so numb
I've got lungs of tar
I think I'm dumb
I wish I could reach you, star
That hot car fumed
13 forever
I am torn by a fresh wound
Liam + death forever
Liam Zevoughn 9/16/18

OASIS

I am bleeding
But that's okay
Still breathing
So much to say
I saw your heart harden
My sunshine lays
In soil bays
I watched you in the garden
I need you today
If I stare, pardon
You move in such a sinister sort of way
Take me by the wrist
Do me my one wish today
You are bliss
Please say this
"You are my oasis."
You grew in sun rays
My sunshine lays
In soil bays
Liam Zevoughn 9/28/18

BAILEY

Come back
Leave a light on
I am spilling all my guts
I am killing all these musts
So give back what I took away
Because I can't find it
O, to live as a void; look away
I think I am in love
I didn't have the courage to say
That I was afraid
I will regret it tomorrow
& every day
Liam Zevoughn 5/10/18

QUEEN

She was a brave queen
I was preadolescent
I am but a slave to the free & a servant to nicotine
& we could have lessened
Our own sorrow
She wore a tiara
This could not wait for tomorrow, I miss you Sierra
Liam Zevoughn 5/19/18

PAINT

The pure I taint
I have no complaint
With sinners & alcoholics I acquaint
The cure
The cure happens to me when I paint
Though I taint the pure no idea can hold restraint
I am cursed
To love oils
More than flesh
I will leave in a hearse as society boils
The paint stays fresh
These colors are absolute
It is the faithful I pollute
Liam Zevoughn 5/25/18

CANVAS

God, please find the dark
Upon my heart; tell me where my band is & hand this
God, I am your canvas
Only I can fit this
Unique
Please paint away my sickness
I am a freak
& this
Is perfect
God, I am your canvas
Ever so faintly
Please
Please, paint me
Hark this:
I am ill
Please find the darkness
Here's to hope you will hand this
God, I am your canvas
Liam Zevoughn 6/3/18

MELANCHOLY BIRD

When I heard
I thought I was in Hell
I could tell I was wrong
A melancholy bird
 Sings a terribly sad song
When I heard
I felt as if this writing was too long
A melancholy bird
 Sings a terribly sad song
Liam Zevoughn 6/3/18

OCEAN

I am free falling
In the motion
You are lulling the sweetest tune
I am in the ocean
& you are a pulling moon
I will drown
In your love
I hope that I will never let you down
This always was
I envy your light
That which blinds me
We do this every night but no one ever finds me
I am so glad I found you
So glad to hear the motion
You lull the sweetest tune
I will drown in your ocean
I love you, dearest moon
Liam Zevoughn 6/5/18

Injustice

I yearn for equality
Lady Liberty is not blind
Injustice is all I see
With agony I awake to find
A race
Which still are not free
This place
Has not liberty
But injustice
This race still runs on toughness
& to my amazement
This is absurd
As if they are still in enslavement
They are murdered
This place
Has not liberty
For there is an entire race
Which still are not free
Liam Zevoughn 7/5/18

SCRUTINY

Many nights I awake
To a looming hell
Plenty stable mind at stake
I feel I live in a cell
Any fable time will fake
I ain't living well
God, bless the paranoid
Police scrutinize & destroy the pure
Intent for giving fell
Homies fled from the eyes which toy with her
I send for a risen shell
I awake to a looming hell, see
I await peace of mind to see what relentless scrutiny has done to me
Liam Zevoughn 5/31/17

FIRST SONG

All this I say for you to know
Your beautiful heart's vacancy
Is sewn
Look how my own space has graced God's seed & grown
Liam Zevoughn 7/15/18

MUSE

I am bemused with sadness
I want to go & hide
Don't want to go inside because I am confused by madness
I miss the tide
My mind is composite
I don't care
All my love & strength I deposit
So long live the demon in my closet
I'm too scared to get out there
I send my love with this carrier
Do not lose
I do admit with this barrier I am bemused
I only muse
Liam Zevoughn 7/25/18

PAY

Pay
This is their song again
My hand on this quill kills my will everyday
I attest this is true
I confess I have nothing to say
But you
Are the color
I never knew
Such a hue
I could not believe
I hail the beauty from which love was conceived
I would breathe
If only with your consent
I would leave
Only to express my beautiful lament
Only to confess
My heart is bent
Every pump is a blunder
O, I ponder death
One last cigarette & the streets will take me under
Only one step
This life is wrong
Is what I say
Pay, pay, pay
This is their song again
Liam Zevoughn 7/26/18

Shine

I want to talk
But you won't even text me
Nothing new
Truth is I miss you while you're standing right next to me
I miss you
So stand in my sights again
Understand in these nights
I weep with this pen
I command
I hope these silent fights
Will never end
Place your hand in mine
Never have I felt
Such divine
Never have i dealt
Such shine
Liam Zevoughn 8/5/18

SEVERITY

When I reached the bottom
I found nothing
In the bright colors of autumn
I wish I had something
Of all the highs
Still I am blue
I even died
& still I love you
So to the demon
I surrender
Hot tar
I can't remember if I'm supposed to be this far
Assure me, dear star
Beautiful ember
That this may be the last disparity
Cure my scars
& their sickening severity
I reached for books & I got them
I loved the car's hot heat
Then I reached the bottom
Dear star, I tire of a heartbeat
Liam Zevoughn 8/14/18

Legitimacy

So sweet intricacy
I call to you in distress
The earth gives & I swear to you Nirvana lives
My everything is a mess
Let there be no fault
For the burden endeavored
Let the green of trees consult & hold their secrets forever
I am constantly hurt by a clock
Now & then
I am free to be but
I am comforted by 2Pac
Sweet poetry
With this I sever
I listen woefully for I know you have been gone for an ever
Let these words be only legitimacy
I long for rest
So sweet intricacy
My everything is a mess
I hold on to maybe
I hope the Lord would be gracious enough to save me
Liam Zevoughn 11/13/18

HARNESS

Dear room
Vacancy
I've cut myself a wound
They can't see
If I could only mend
Oh, my feeling is coming back again
Love be to thee
My love I send
This despair takes
I've made my own mistakes
Hark this:
I've been dead
Dead but not alive I thrive in darkness
Far behind he left my mother
Heartless cheats
Tar I find hard to smother
My heart beats for another
Harmless defeats
So dear vacancy,
Clutch me like a harness
They can't see me in pain
I am only an artist
I shall crawl back to my den
Dear pain in my heart,
Oh, my feeling is coming back again
Liam Zevoughn 10/14/18

DREAMING II

I am dreaming
I caught wind
Of your scent
I mean
I thought
You were heaven sent
I planted a seed
That only grew
Forgive me
I am lost
If I only knew
You breathe innocence
Too
Would make sense
The seed grew
& told fables
This tree was able
This tree was constantly
Unstable
But still held to ground
At last I had found
A partner worth saving
But fast in my departure
I cried for the seed was engraving
A tombstone
Of significance
Of my own flesh & bone
Which read "I cannot live for my impotence."
& this I should have known
For no everlasting tree could love flesh & bone
I awake to find panic & distress on my own
Maybe I should take my own medicine
Won't you be heaven sent?
Curse my worn skeleton

But for a moment I caught wind of your scent
Symbolic of meaning
I want a break
Please agree
So, I am dreaming
Please don't wake me
Liam Zevoughn 12/1/18

Nicotine

It is in
In my skin
Forcing a tide that's sane
The nicotine
Coursing through my veins
Such vanity
& if not
I am pushed to insanity
I am a fiend
Dear nicotine,
You have destroyed me once again
You are much faster than I
Such comfort in our disaster but I
Think you're my friend
The high I cannot resist
With every sigh I feel kissed
By sin
So dear nicotine
You're in
In my skin
Liam Zevoughn 12/20/18

EMILEE

But the silence hurts me
A crisis in the calm
I am at my device's mercy
She is a beautiful fawn
I can see?
She is a song & her name is Emilee
For her, beyond the tomb
A girl I adore
Today, I must say, never kill innocence in a womb
How could one want more?
She is a fawn; idle
A dove
How can you claim love when you are so homicidal?
Look above
How could you hurt her?
This is what I say
But your relief is a only a murder away
Absurd, you dream of God
But your actions speak louder today
& she awaits me in heaven
Only one God I praise
Let me learn you a lesson just ask miss Emmons; I support
love & grace
I want to hit that resin but my beliefs hold in place
This baby doesn't cry so throw her away
How sad
You can't claim love when you can't let her stay
Today, I must say
No one lives only for themself anyway
Liam Zevoughn 1/22/19

BLONDE HAIR

Blonde hair
Your complexion bemuses me
I thought you weren't even there
No sprightly lore could have confused me
Like you
Your delicate skin
Is pristine in such a way
I couldn't speak in
The nimbus in which you stay
Blonde hair
I know not
Your name
Standing there
I am lost in your golden fame
Blonde hair, I want you to say
I'll be okay
Without you
I want you to stay
Sun rays are about you
This connection excused everything
Every land
I dream of thee
Your complexion bemuses me, please understand
How greatly you inspire
In your pristine sea
I caught fire
& lastly
You are pristine
I would take your hand gladly
Liam Zevoughn 1/19/19

ALIVE

I feel like an angel
Ain't much to say
I said yesterday's angles don't define me today
Keep going I think this is the right way
Today I gave God a call
No reply
I said I cracked my head & landed on the asphalt

My body is an empty shell
What should this mean?
I said I had a dream I was going to Hell
In this dream I was dying all the way
Crying for life
Sobbing constantly for Jesus Christ
What else could you say?

There is only one with such power
Dear procession, this is my confession
I had a dream I ascended into heaven
Me & other children picked flowers
& spirits we tried to leaven
& stayed together
In Christ alive
& this was forever; an eternal thrive
Liam Zevoughn 1/29/19

Numb

I need to feel
I need to hurt
To be real
I must burn
The more feeling I lose
The better off I am
No longer do I feel a bruise from touch of hands
Words come off my tongue
In pieces
What I will become when
All feeling ceases
Is numb
It comes
Time creases
Just as soon
As my consciousness
Releases
LZDD

PERENNIAL

Why does my heart still beat
When my body continues to decompose
Why do I continue to eat when all is disposed
Why do I stay conscious
While every memory fades
Why stay in hospice while unresponsive go to the grave
Life is sinful
Nothing great could ever last
Why is it only hate is perennial but never the grass
I live in these words but never have response
Will renaissance ever answer these burdens with which I carry on
What does depart mean?
The revival of art is only a dream
LZDD

THE CAGE

Can you imagine what it's like to be locked in a cage
Like an animal in a zoo
You cannot turn the page
The only person is you
Your expressions are only as far as your incapable mind
Your body is limited too
The rage inside is the only friend
The lion roars but you can only apologize again
People stare but don't get too close
And then you are alone with the rose
Above the birds mock
But my love isn't empty
They are the lock
Only God can judge me
LZDD

Eyes Shut

We close our eyes before we pray
Even though our ties with God have gone astray
We close our eyes before we kiss
Even when the night fades into day
Without our sight we can feel untainted bliss
With our eyes closed we can even hide the dark away
Cover it up and pretend it isn't there
Until the sun shines we defend and prepare
We close our eyes before we feel pain
Scared
& then we feel the pull
It's insane; don't fight it
Blinded we can feel that it's beautiful
Tightened from the world but
We see as we feel
With our eyes shut
We can feel what is real
LZDD

Exit Sign

Turn off the sirens they do not scare me
I am worthless, like my life, isn't it
Free me because my mind cannot bare imprisonment

Leave me alone here I am blind
If I die with music I will be at peace (angels cried)
These feelings are too much I will mentally perform suicide

I must have a purpose
At times I wonder my existence
What really is my true service?
I trust few, and those with great resistance

The exit sign taunts me with lights
It knows what's beyond
The demon in me fights because this life is wrong; but the show
must go on

I remember the clouds & ever color of the rainbow
I was sent back here
God feared I was not ready to go
LZDD

AUGUST

I only sink
The waters were tested
Dear somebody, I think, again, you have left me arrested
If you can only know
The pain in my eyes
The music would only grow
Completely satisfied
By a speeding car
I was faded
Death by blunt force
But I'm back, reincarnated
Breath by shunt indorse
But I'll be okay
Despite the rugged coarse
Is that what you want me to say?
I am a walking corpse today
The shunt has been severed
Honest
I promise I can only give you a forever
Says the warm summer month of August
Somebody + Liam forever
Liam Zevoughn 8/6/18

PROTECTION

Give ear to this
The more I live
The more it's serious
I know you're alive
But can't we simply thrive?
Excuse the thread
Depression arrives
I know you are alive but I am dead
I wanted affection
In life
But for your protection I'll stay on ice
A brutal cold to which I have no deflection
I died
But still yearn for affection
Can you tell me why
I haven't the slightest detection
Of interest
I am so wry but yearn for complexion in the simplest
Excuse the thread
I am dead
I yearn for connection
Maybe even fame
Is it my turn for affection?
For your protection I won't use your name
Liam Zevoughn 8/5/18

INSPIRE

I would give it all up
If I could go back home
I could live it all up
Just to destroy these bones
Just to, once again, taste death
It's sweet motion
I want to end & face rest
No more to be in commotion
O, Lord, the last syllable that leaves my lips
Let it inspire
Let my breath seethe to the tips of fire
This sweet sound be so dire
With these words I conspire
I struggle with survival
Not with remorse
Trouble is I'd rather die on the Bible
At least I have one resource
O, that sweet motion
Death, you have won my heart
I will show you devotion even in the morning in the dark
I want to leave this place without a goodnight
Or farewell
I want to be in space where I can hold tight
Without this shell
Prison
What can you do while living in hell but hold to religion
Sing to me a spell
I cannot be destined to fire
God has my heart
Let my last breath to death inspire
Liam Zevoughn 7/18/18

Flower's Pollen

I am calling to say that I love you
I'm calling to say if an earthly prophecy is true
In a few weeks we will be gone
In less time earth seeks to mourn its last dawn
My dear friend, I have faith
But have fallen
My dear, we are safe
But cannot confide in flower's pollen
I pray your return
My dear friend, we have but little time
In rhymes, my ardent thoughts, they burn
Nearest the end is such brittle twine
I love you
Tender & lovingly I embrace breeze of the sea
If an early prophecy is true
Let it be
We love
So have not fallen
Soon we shall ascend from the flower's pollen
LZDD

FEEL ME

Who started me?
My soul is old but not faded
Surrender me, poverty
But I'm back, reincarnated
In awe & shocked at the way God made it
She is dark hearted but not seen
Who started me?
I'm back, reincarnated
She saw the real me & darted
Can you feel me?
I'm back, reincarnated
Truth is I love the real me
God, can you feel me?
Too late
I'm started
Back, reincarnated
Liam Zevoughn 6/3/18

PROPHECY

I am new
Honestly
I am too
2Pac's prophecy
Lord, can you seal me?
Like a letter for the better
God, can you feel me?
I came from the gutter
From the deepest street
Did I stutter? I said long live the rose from concrete
& his perfect timing
I cry & no one cares why
Please come out of hiding
I know it's hard to be
I know I'm rapping when I say this
I am the prophecy
2Pac, with the Lord, we pray for the faithless
I know you were conflicted
Ancient history
I know what you were missing but I'm here now
Let there be no mystery
The way I live is an oddity
What else can I say?
I am the prophecy
2Pac, we need you today
Liam Zevoughn 2/1/19

Fog

In the face of fog
Clear
By the grace if God I am here
& ardent words remain
Let me go
Hard to cure
I am heard, so
Pour me down the drain
In the face of fog
Fear
By the grace of God I am here
Will I forever be trapped?
Insanity
Still I stay strapped
Because I need to feed my family
In the face of fog
Be sincere
Because by the grace of God you are here
& read this
If you did so in fear
Dismiss
If you did so in awareness
Thrive
I wrote this in fairness so, please, stay alive
Make it through
I've run out of poetic ways to say I love you
Liam Zevoughn 1/31/19

OBSTACLES

It must be your skin
That which I felt
This pain I'm in
For so long I've dealt
& this pain
Shall be forever
So vain when all you seek is a sever
Please, grow to sail, sis
Love I have failed to resist
Is a life for me probable?
Won't someone say this
"My love exceeds all obstacles."
You are my oasis
Liam Zevoughn 10/27/18

Son

I don't want my son
To suffer
If I ever found the one
I would not want them to grow tougher
For me
My greatest fear
Is to be aimlessly floating in the atmosphere
My one seed
I condemn thee to a life of being free
& forever
I shall seal me
& shall live on
God, can you feel me?
A battalion
I don't want my son
To suffer
If I could only find your mother
If she could only hear
The small lament I mutter
I am so forlorn
But free
Read this when I am better
This is a letter to my unborn seed
Liam Zevoughn 2/27/19

CONFINEMENT

Confinement
How I cherish thee
It's just the sign meant
"This way you may see."
Confinement
Bring me
By the sea
Sing to me
The perspective
Confinement
I cannot fathom
Confinement
Let me breathe
With this enthusiasm
I will flourish beneath
Liam Zevoughn 3/6/19

Falling

But in our falling
We were gracious
I am stalling-remember-this hurts
This empty room is spacious
The moon races-surrender whispers
Don't die but live this
This is a stitch
To fight is vain-tonight I bestow forgiveness
This is a stance to stitch
A chance to flourish
My pen falls with a thud
To taint is to sin
Tonight I paint in blood-that's how much love I'm in
That old quill is calling
Defying
But in our falling
Live every day like you're dying
Liam Zevoughn 10/26/19

The Pianist

The pianist awaits one to applaud
He contemplated fleeing
The realest thing I ever got high on was God
Most music is too freeing

So flee
Find the pain to once you mused
A hypnotic tree
Your time was morbidly enthused

You see the pianist flew
In his dreams to intricate steps in a fog
Say it's morbid too He murdered those notes
The realest I ever got high on was God
The pulpit never votes but rest easy because the pianist was too odd
Liam Zevoughn 8/9/19

DENIAL

Meanwhile
Prison for awhile
While you're laying tile
Jimmy, there's a difference between skepticism and total denial
Liam Zevoughn 8/14/19

EMPATHETIC

Empathetic
I remember this deja vu
So pathetic when the only one I dream of is you
Liam Zevoughn 8/16/19

THIEVES

You didn't know Christ existed
Hang your head
Jack, do you think they would have understood had you persisted?
This I sang instead
Of triumph
& to resist famed silence of the dead
You are inspiring
This came like violence in the red
True electric wiring
Graced your mind
& now the pressure is faced with an opening to find
& your bones fisted
Life was said
You didn't know Christ existed so hang your head
May the kiln that is your heart glow
Blessed are those who don't see & believe
Festered woes won't be conceived
Now you know
May the choir be thieves
Liam Zevoughn 9/11/19

I Broke My Own Heart
in the Theater

Now I find those flowers were meat eaters
I broke my own heart in the theater
I breathe only for understanding
I can't leave & that is for every planning
I found blood along the riverbank feature
Wrong?
Profound godly dust must have sung a song because I broke my
own heart in the theater
How could one have such flawless tact?
How could one even know what to say?
I just like to act
But who lives to be toyed with anyway?
In a dream, what is wrong?
We are a silly creature
Profound godly dust has a song because I broke my own heart in
the theater
Liam Zevoughn 9/15/19

FEEBLE MIND

My feeble mind
Cannot take the pressure
The easel this time
Is out to uphold for the lesser

& as we drove into the blinding sun
I am fine to be
There isn't need to run because the trees are looking at me

Such a dreamlike blue
Can you see?
The trees aren't looking at me they're looking at you

May they move past a violent rage
For the better
May they watch as you take your time on stage forever

The easel this time
Has eluded me
My feeble mind
Has rooted thee
Liam Zevoughn 9/23/19

EDEN

Blades of grass are killed
When will you surrender the first frost?
Lord, I will
I will follow you to the cross

& this was true
Needn't argue
I dreamed of the Lord in hues I could not believe
I just want to scream I love you too much to leave

I needn't a stone
To cut myself on
Being alone is a hell of its own

My personal garden of Eden
Was waiting for me all along
Still, long live the demon
I find that God's creation was never wrong

Angels in white robes
I awaited thee
No danger, so
Help me be free
Liam Zevoughn 9/29/19

THYME

I don't know what I'm doing
Why am I breathing
Why am I moving
Why do I keep winning when I plan on losing
I recall singing, to you, a song
After all this bringing
I feel a slumber would be too long
Bring me time
In return
Sing to me with thyme
While inside I shall burn
Insidious & low
With the sun I am wooing
So no I don't know what I'm doing
Liam Zevoughn 10/22/19

IMMINENT

I reminisce on the doom of fall
I do not ask why
Do not cry at my funeral
The heartache that was to be
Is shrouded
Let thy be not clouded
Youth-how sweet to see
Truth is dying is fun for me
This fume has gone far-to the key
Let the moon & stars comfort thee
This end is soon for all
Do not cry at my funeral
My breath is stealing
Even if I could I would never circumvent
I can't help feeling My death is imminent
Liam Zevoughn 10/29/19

WISHES

I'm so sick of wishes
Anemic screams
I used to think raindrops were angel kisses
Bulimic fiends
I used to say I love you
Shrouded veils
Please, stay true
Follow the rails & find me brand new
Paint filled pails
Today I used you to express
Tainted tales
Bruised through some new flesh & confessed
The tired man fishes
& the lake is dead
I'm so sick of wishes
Take me instead; raindrops are angel kisses
They just graced my head
Liam Zevoughn 11/3/19

ALEX

Mightier than pride
Humble
I may whisper a stutter or mumble but I cried
When I witnessed omnipotence
& the one upon the cross that died
Was God fixated with the affects?
I was lost but returned like a tide
The cutest thing God created was Alex
Could you tell me why?
Who I was ten minutes ago
Was another
Though the love I defend is sprightly
I never know
The foe that treads lightly
Will not ever grow
The sky may wake & rumble but I say unto thee never fake but stay humble
Liam Zevoughn 11/23/19

YOUNG LOVE

Hung doves
Here is uncertainty
Reminiscing on young love
Sheer thrill
I was
Fear
My parents killed
My other half
& now I have grown
I went & filled my soul with grass & Lord I have known
Fear
A hung dove
Will not suppress me here
Young love
You are fearsome
Young love you are deadly
Hear some scripts & try to debunk
But I need steady
I'm sunk already
Lung of
Tar
Young love
You are too far
Liam Zevoughn 11/26/19

FORGIVENESS

This ain't a short story
Just a vile sin
Let's begin where you left me in purgatory
I can't win

This ain't a short story
But I am lost for words
When you left me gory & without birds
I suffered with your tee that was absurd

Just a vile sin
Leave me again & you will be left
Why do I try to begin
All I've ever known is your rejection

This ain't a short story
My mind now sways
You left me in purgatory but how gracious are the angels to kiss me anyway
Liam Zevoughn 12/8/19

STAGE

This was more than a phase
A birth right
I was born for the stage
But Jesus took me by the night

More than a phase
A destiny much unpaved
A boy once born for the stage has now frayed
Liam Zevoughn 12/30/19

Vanity

I can't help but call
Can you tell me why I'm here
Sweet vanity
Hell won't swallow all
But you should fear
Take me to insanity
To this I am sworn
Fate sees a broken family
& I am torn
Your intricate steps have left me craving more
But forlorn
I have torn every resident from their home
Graving your beautiful little tone
And insanity
You are & always was
So sweet vanity
For you I have no love
Lost is every larking tot
But crossing that empty parking lot
I experienced such hues
The fight isn't over I'm just blue
I love my family
A strength that will not fall
So sweet vanity, I can't help but call
Liam Zevoughn 1/6/20

INDIFFERENCE

It rinses away my purity
Makes sense
My indifference is everything & I love obscurity
This euphoria is heaven sent

I am not a fighter
I've not a soul
The weight of the world feels lighter
Long live this duo

Neighbors have not a fence
Of this I'm sure
Long live my indifference
I could finish but I don't care anymore
Liam Zevoughn 11/20/19

TRACING

my ode
Is soft
I'm having another episode so loft
Another burn
I'm smoking human remains
So to dust you shall return because time is choking & tames
My ode
Another episode
Gather round
She is tracing
She'd rather go down but God spoke her as pacing
This tale is so old
Does this end in disaster?
My ode is another episode but I hope she reaches me faster
Liam Zevoughn 1/25/20

ANGELS

Some burn
Their wings crushed with ash
They discern
May God heal their wrath
They fly
In a nimbus unbeknown
They cry
They fit this unsown
Frame
They may fight
They may say Jesus is Lord for a night but they still are the same
& so I declare
The angels at my death
I miss you
Is this fair?
I'll use all my breath just to cry for your hue & virtue
When will you learn?
Diffuse this issue; in depth I shy from the angel which burns
Liam Zevoughn 2/25/20

LANGUAGE OF THE ANGELS

My own will dangles
I'm just a kid
But I do remember when I spoke the language of the angels
& all the sobbing I did
Amounted to making myself

It's true to understand
True to be
It's seems to me the wounded have the upper hand
& the empty

I doubt any are sane
& He was raised
I don't want to be erased; our motivation is the same
Liam Zevoughn 3/8/20

GENESIS

I'll take the booth on the right
This is a dream
Truth is I need sight
What can this mean?

You are out of my league
But I can't withstand the dark
You are bliss; I have loved you from the start
I was more than flirting with Genesis but we broke apart

The occasion arose but there was an end
True
I drew myself closer to your friend
Just to be close to you

& the taste of you
Is unfathomable
You meant to stay
But our arguments about the sun led astray

I want to tell the world about my elation
Truth is long ago I fell in love with creation
Liam Zevoughn 3/17/20

FLESH

For them
I keep a poem
In my guitar strings
No one even thought they bought the tar
It just stings
& so this brings bliss, too
The youth will sing
I miss you

Let's get by this test
No sorrow
If I crucify my flesh I will live to see tomorrow

Who should know?
As far as East runs by West
The feeling should be mutual & I will crucify my flesh
Liam Zevoughn 3/18/20

Ambition

Smiling faces
Put me down
Formidable, fearful places
Threw me around

Ambition
I knew you once
Now shrouded in fear
I wanted the chance to dance on tee but no one can see me here
through my PTSD

fragrance of
Lavender
This will inspire
Pages after pages of disaster
I will start a fire

A song too long
Please, do part
Please Forgive
Long live my car crash heart
No place I lived compared
To God's chariot
I will find this faulty wire & bury it

The fire which inspired me
Still burns today
& with grace I will erase the burdens which weighed so I can
finally stay
Liam Zevoughn 3/21/20

GARDEN OF SPARKS

Dear star
Release an ode to this
Perhaps a cure?
I know this is pure hopelessness
But my pen does not deter

Dear star
I think there are spies
Garden of sparks
Some if not all of you are lies
Do not harden your hearts

I've had my fair share on hints
But I'm not dumb
And I'm not done trying to convince
I can't feel my lungs
What will become of this?

In my den of marks
I found you
A garden of sparks
I will push through
Liam Zevoughn 3/21/20

PSYCHOPATHY

Some dulled too far
But I am fine
I found my ticket to hallelujah boulevard
My chance to shine

Stop and see
I can not control psychopathy
Liam Zevoughn 3/24/20

SPADE

A deep spade
Killed
I'm so afraid of free will
A voice, shrill
I will fade
This is God's will
This is today
Deep in the earth
Is a forlorn presence
Weeping is heard
& what for it's residents?
It would be easy if they could kill
Again
I'm so afraid of free will
Send
A blessing
Hark this darkness but yearn forever
Nesting is scary
Spark this but burn & sever
My best to Gary
Take that spade & fill
My heart
I'm so afraid of free will
So afraid to be in the dark
Liam Zevoughn 3/26/20

RAY

I ask why
Do possessions
Get clotted in the mind
Even thy old transgressions He blotted out with signs
& even the weary spied but this was a blunder
& even the teary eyed can expect wonders
Thine heart was cast away
But truly I tell you
This dark shall fade & truth shall stay
Yearning eternally
For a better understanding
Burning infernally; will thy forever be empty handed?
At mention of thy name
I will fumble
Detention in the game never looked so vain
I don't want to stumble
& so I ask why
Can thy give a reason?
I am castaway
Understand I don't wish godly treason I just want to ray
Liam Zevoughn 3/28/20

DIRE

As you tee
I'd like to reminisce
Are you another casualty?
Fly us over this
Virus which seems to sober kids
Seems to destroy
& What dreams of joy
If it ends
No more sublime, in the meantime I'm saying goodbye to all
my friends

As you flee
I want to inspire
Are you another casualty?
Can we outlast this fire?
What illness can we fake?
Let us conspire
& leave a footprint in its wake
Was anything else this dire?
Liam Zevoughn 4/8/20

Excuses

& the godly
Seem to spy on us
Darn my body
Of this virus

The tar takes its toll
Of all hindsight endeavors
Lauren, you take arise & prize the meek & small for the better

I must say you are divine; no doubt
You can be not vague but always fine
If this plague ends I'd like to ask you out

Of all excuses & buts I must say I haven't the guts
To say a word
Of all muses & cuts
I move further toward forlorn
This pen abuses the ups & downs but for you it grows pro-
found & worn

& I will drown another issue
This fuses the musts
I just want to say I miss you
There are too many excuses & buts
Liam Zevoughn 3/29/20

LILITH

You shall return to dust
This song reminds me of you, Lilith
Do fall upon the urn; you must
You were so wrong but it's you I want to be with
He spoke in dust
Your own determination put you in Hell
How formidable
Yet her imagination lie in a deep well
Now, the Lord did not fable
Now you're in a cell
Now I am torn for the creature I desire inspired from clay is down
where I cannot reach
Where does she lay?
Few fall & turn to us
You shall return to dust
I foresaw a life
Void of all restrictions
I called you wife
We joyed free of affliction
Too small to learn to trust
You shall return to dust
So I heard muttered by a grapevine
Absurd moths fluttered & I took mine
Dew, I yearn to bust
You shall return to dust
This quill is with
Us
I love you, Lilith
You shall return to dust
Liam Zevoughn 4/1/20

Madison

Had it been that long ago I had beheld thee?
I figured you were trying to rub salt in my wounds
I'm sad when I tell myself it's just me
Madison
My sunshine lays
In soil bays
Add a sun
We have crossed the threshold, saved
I think I'm dumb
Can we mesh? & though the road is unpaved we are numb
so it's okay
& the sand dunes
Fell on me
I figured you were trying to rub salt in my wounds
Had it been that long ago I beheld thee?
So I just stayed & waited
Frayed & Spaded
Decayed & faded
I will take this created mandated form
& express
I won't fake this belated storm of creative hopelessness
Something so clear for you too see
Give an ode to this; had it been that long ago I beheld thee?
Liam Zevoughn 4/5/20

QUEEN II

Lauren, it's you I mention
With lungs of tar
Hopefully you wrote me off as divine intervention
As a star
& so my implication is set then
So it mildly seems
But in my wildest dreams I do see you again
May you deem me as wild
May you intervene
The stage I seen when I was only a child
Led me to a queen
Whose control of the soul is divine
But the bruises & cuts wore in
I will lose hold to find the vine
I will use this to shine on Lauren
Liam Zevoughn 4/7/20

GARDEN

Lavender after rose
Painting
My ever after knows
Eventually I will have to quit tainting
Waiting
For a line to strike me the same way
Fading
Let's pour some time over it, today
With open eyes
I will wonder into your garden
& not know why
Still sunburnt farther than skin
True elatedness
Sheer brilliance at any time you could come in
Strewed, belated kiss
I always awaited this
Have to deter the future throws
Rain stings
Lavender after rose
Painting
Here's for my heart to harden
& for yours to specify
I will wonder into your garden
& not know why
Liam Zevoughn 4/9/20

GROUP

I see you
I can't tell if it's faux
But I spent all this time wishing you would grow
I do wonder if your seed would start to sow
My rabbit went over the ocean
How fond; such a habit to watch the currents motions
Vagabond's certain devotion
This will inspire
Rag made of the sun, enough commotion, this is a fire
I am ablaze so stand nearby and watch me work around the dire
Since I traced the first basketball hoop
I have enjoyed this wire
I have enjoyed my time in group
We are hired to make this small place brighter
Words come off my tongue in fractions
I knew I came to you because I need distraction
Liam Zevoughn 4/13/20

Coincidental Love

Refer to the above header
Coincidence is not divine
After a while I wrote this love letter
I do wish you were mine
Never doubt this is pure
I am grey but I'll never say I wrote this about any particular
I won't say who it's for
Can anybody see?
I'm old
I'm saying everybody bleeds but who can tell me the story of the
cardinal on the marigold?
& so I wrote
Without a destination
I devoted all time to a song that, to me, was creation
Intricately sewn on your heart
Was a warning
& now my ghost haunts the dark
I am lost every morning
I am the used, the sold
Attuned but bold
I'm saying everybody bleeds but who can tell me the story of the
cardinal on the marigold?
Liam Zevoughn 4/14/20

DOPE FIENDS

I will not give up my moral
Feel the reeling today
Even when you shut the world out, girl, it's adorable
I guess it's true: real feelings don't go away
Spies
I see you
Even when my back is turned I can sympathize
But I wouldn't want to be you
Just let me be pure
Let me be mysterious
The cure is my medicine
Call me Mr. delirious; the best for my skeleton
Every bone in its place
How gracious is youth
Truth is I am alone & practically useless
Glowing to a dim, warm hue
Flowing & honing
Form me with glue
Going & going is my mind on marijuana residue
& so it seems my bones may never circumvent this torture
There goes my dreams
Imminent for
Dope fiends
Definite scenes will scratch the seams
But never disagree when I say the high won't be like the sun
which gleams
Liam Zevoughn 4/16/20

Optimism

On the gurney
Your heart spilled it's guts
You can't hurt me anymore it's just excuses & buts
My part in this masquerade
Was to watch you cry
We both asked to stay but you were wry
So now I won't be dismal
This pull to optimism will not be quenched
Dull is my pencil
I watched as you wrenched
I've never been more alive
Arise for a better thrive
Dive forever but you will not arrive
On this journey
There were not cuts
On the gurney
Your heart spilled it's guts
Liam Zevoughn 4/17/20

NEUROPATHY

May your soul dream a sound neuropathy
No issues
Uncontrolled psychopathy
I miss you
Liam Zevoughn 4/18/20

PROLONG

Rob my dreams & these
Creeps
I hear obscenities when I try to sleep
Rinse away my illness
The creep which seeps
Heard this today but didn't stop the realest
Absurd are those who say
Words are but only feelings
& so I prolong
O, the endurance
Never doubt this song
But always cure the sure of purest hearts
In ways, I guess, I lure the furious dark
I fade the best & deter curious stars
Laid & confessed is her delirious Tzars
& so rob my dreams
Today
Take away the gravest fiends
Are they seeing these?
Deep
Still I hear obscenities when I try to sleep
Liam Zevoughn 4/29/20

If I Die 2night

For tight reasons
I will not circumvent
If I die 2night-my death is imminent
I call it treason to escape to youthful veins
I crawl to wheezing states
Truthful rains
Erased all the pain
Fake & conspire
Ditches
I remember you but all witches are going to the lake of fire
No riches
No desires
I wish to only do right in eyes unmatched
So if I die 2night forget the lies & let freedom catch
My soul
Though I do no right for thee yet, flies become that eerie sense
of despair
Throw the bouquet anyway
You will never find me there
A bow too tight is a blunder
If I do die 2night remember me in the thunder
If I fall in a crease in paper
In fruitful vanity
I call it treason to escape to youthful veins
Insanity, I know you and I were tight
Surrender to birds
If I die 2night remember my words
Liam Zevoughn 5/6/20

Rough & Vicious

What spirit could rule this
Temple
I was once young & foolish
Now stricken, I am mental

I discern her breath
Just alright
But this flame could scorch me to death
Must be light

Must be surreptitious
Must be insane
Rough & vicious to the lame
Is ignorance always in vain?
Is all vanity fair when you know there is someone who can't do
the same ?

What spirit could rule this
Vessel
I was young & foolish but now with a pain I wrestle
Liam Zevoughn 5/15/20

THE SCREAMS OF A LATENCY

Vanity
See
Dear Bailey V., if you truly saw my side you would agree
To conceive something so precious, some lose or run on tee
To leave nothing by extracting their roots from a tree
Vanity
Be
Hear the screams of a latency
Let them by
Divine intervention belated me but who knows the scream of the
butterfly?
Liam Zevoughn 5/16/20

Dead Veins

Breathe
Snide remarks
What to do when your insides are dry leaves
You come apart
The poise I rally
Can not compare
Dear Sally, can you feel that there?
Down in the valley you rake your thyme
Around the alley, the dead trees make you time
Another gown for tally, so much that once shined
You tend to dally, dead veins compose your insides
You put me to sleep, rolling rocker
I'll stay
I wasn't invented by a controlling doctor but the way
You breathe
Snide remarks
Smothered, weeded graveyards will weave
As for me, I will sew you a heart
I'm afraid you have a need
But the feeling was there all along, you perfect seed
Red rains or simple beads?
Sally, your dead veins are formidable, by all means
I hardly ditched the hospital's file
But you
I understand your impossible, stitched smile
Liam Zevoughn 5/17/20

(Insert Image 1)

White Moth

White moth
Like a white flame
Summers brought you to me again
These pills are hard to swallow
Night of cloth
I remember when there was no white moth to follow
So much cost
Creativity
I know you well
This moment is to me what heroin is to fiends
The veins tell
See
Life in jail ain't for me, no penitentiary
I am of what use?
Foamy broth
These pills are hard to swallow, I am lost
Only toss
I remember when there was no white moth to follow
& the patio he crossed
Living his best reflection
Giving me any and all sense of direction
Wings of blinding dust
What to be
I call for thee, this is a must
Liam Zevoughn & Brittany 5/21/20

BIRDCAGE CHEST

Absurd rage is not best
The darkened is many
In my birdcage chest, I cannot fit too many
I heard it, lest you don't understand
In case you won't lend a hand
Word to the page that whispered finesse
I cannot fit too many inside my birdcage chest
Sure as sage I will cleanse the window of quest
& search for wire that makes me confused
We're in a cage
But today I say, we're fire in the hearts of those that lose
Liam Zevoughn 5/23/20

HONEST TONES

Behold the Lord, for I lie not
Enough for nobody
As thunder spans, you must understand
The thought is spurred
I once was godless & absurd
Odd is
The melancholy bird
Wanting, haunting, forever forgetting the word
Honest tones
I won't be a godless sewn
Hypocrite
I will not taunt this
Still not grown, my own gift is an ode that fits
I told them for I despise rot
Behold the Lord, for I lie not
Liam Zevoughn 5/23/20

WRITHE

Spitting the truth
Rawest word
I love you youth or grace?
None would worry If you could see the Lord's place
Here's for me to writhe
And you to muster anew
Look me in the eyes, I'm telling you the truth
Liam Zevoughn 5/25/20

Aneurysm

May God bleed dry this prison
Whispered apostasies
Music induced brain aneurysm; a kiss to the rotten sea
It bent me
See, I never found something so empty
Now I am tarred
Now I am scarred to the father who sent me
A long song to the daughter which welt me
Stay calm, for Christ is risen
Okay to the odd who leaves "why" written
And not spoke
May God bleed dry is prison
A wry, burlesque bloke
Liam Zevoughn 5/29/20

DISINTEGRATED CANARY

& on I'll carry
The bold may vary
A lame bird, famous words; I'm trying to tell the story of the dis-
integrated canary
This won't be long
But every song he sang was on tee
Now he's gone
& she laments, honestly
She watched, by day, the apostasy
She hears him say
I haven't use for the rotted
Please see
My body is falling apart, let thy be clotted
& wrong was the defect
Faded & scary
Never wondering about affect I will miss you dear disinte-
grated canary
Liam Zevoughn 5/30/20

Pearl

Only one in the world
For days I have praised about the one sewing me
His gospel unfurled
To the girl who said "I love you" without knowing me
You are a pearl
I was blinded by the sun
Life behind these rungs
Ain't nothing new
With wheezing lungs I say that I love you too
Liam Zevoughn 6/6/20

Stairs

If you could understand my crazy words
You would find peace
Dead baby birds
Their mother still brings food & when will this cease?
Imminent transgressors
I feel you crease
Indefinite obsessor
I was once there
Was this all a test or was it fair?
I'll take the stairs
That she's buying
So rare & definitely bare but I pray that she dares to stop flying
An admirable lady used prosperous words
Be at ease & pleaz
Bury those dead baby birds
Liam Zevoughn 6/15/20

GIVING UP

Well I'm giving up
So wish me luck
I saw those grates
I missed that time
I can certainly tell you soulmates do exist because I found mine

The stare I received
Shall be ingrained
& for me she weaved & stained
The imprint of love so true
I went, I waned, I flew
Present is pain
A latency that seemed to bloom
I fell
& I'll be dragging this anxious mind to Hell

No words compare
Angelic discerning
Every time I think of you we just stare
I've told my bait & now I am burning
My soulmate will have me forever yearning
Liam Zevoughn 6/19/20

REMEDY

Enough of the same
Mentality
I snuffed the flame of reality
Now I live in a frantic state
But never soothed the burn
Forgive & discern your fate
I am looking for the worm that ate
My enemy
I am searching to end me
Would someone darn, I don't mean harm, I need a remedy
Liam Zevoughn 6/26/20

WEAVING

The best feeling in life is to give
I am dreaming; this I will say instead of screaming
When I don't want to live
The lavender is in bloom
& the heavenly free
Have to deter the moon because this is better than 70 degrees
Have to learn the room together; don't reprimand me
Murmur the wrongs
But never doubt without this pen
I could not lull you the sweetest songs
The dead are leaving
I am dreaming, I am dreaming, I am dreaming
Curtly sway
Into me
But I say, today I will start weaving
Anyway
I am dreaming
Liam Zevoughn 6/26/20

DANIELLE'S HEART

The paths in my view
Sometimes I can't tell them
Apart
But would Danielle sing something from her heart?
Liam Zevoughn 7/1/20

My wish

Heed the butterfly's kiss
But I
I need something more than this
Don't I?

I will hold my breath and count to ten
Because I know death is coming for me again

I will utter my wish
Count to ten
I will heed the butterfly's kiss because I know death is coming
for me again
Liam Zevoughn 7/10/20

ABORTED

The way the path looks
Is distorted
The spies are sly but I'm asking why wasn't I aborted
Please say God passed
Some people
With favor they hoarded
Looking for some antidote to this evil
I shy away from the houses that are boarded
What to oblivion?
What to the dire?
What to the lye which cries for the living wire?
Was this rough?
I am warded
Enough is enough I just wanted to know why I wasn't aborted
Liam Zevoughn 7/12/20

PAINTED GARDEN

Why is it hard to tell if one is tainted or hardened?
Believe
I scanned the intricate steps of your painted garden and it bleeds
A fragrance so angelic
Profound sounds of people's awe; this will remain as relics
It's fame tells it's
Lore
I just want someone to woo me like you did before
A love so everlasting
Was this a sever from crashing?
If I stare please wait & pardon
A ticket I need
I scanned the intricate steps of your painted garden and it bleeds
Liam Zevoughn 7/13/20

I LIE NOT

How could you believe something so true
How could you shine so bright
Please know there's nothing I can do
The light blinds my sight
Hold the spot
Behold the Lord
For I lie not
Liam Zevoughn 7/17/20

Angel Dust

This angle must be well
We fight
I don't know what angel dust smells like
But behind that gas station
I was with a friend
I don't mind if that's odd but it's the last case in the end
It made me feel like a god
Of reverence
I applaud & fade
I rise a sunrise
How raw that we swayed into dwindling tides
We dangle on the meniscus of omnipotence
White light
I don't know what angel dust smells like
Take it from us
We won't grow but must feel alive
Liam Zevoughn 7/18/20

Scene

Will this despair outlast?
I am missing the few; cast on me a spell
I remember skipping class & kissing you & Arielle
Will the gain outweigh the pain?
Rave this scene
I'm about to pay again but I miss you, Brave Queen
Liam Zevoughn 7/20/20

JAPANESE BEETLE

I will defend my tee
At all costs
The hardest thing to find was my identity & now I am no longer lost
This may seem odd but death, to me, whispered a gentle subtlety
God, at his best, turned full
My rubble tea cannot compare

My feet on the ground
The relief of dust
How sweet to die by something other than the virus
So profound

I shy from the fallow tree
As for me, I have needs
But my three shadows & me
Believe

Bend your knees
This book is fact
I felt bad because I couldn't save the Japanese beetle on his back
Liam Zevoughn 7/21/20

Key

The key
Music had me wrapped around its sweet symphonies
What do I mean?
I said the angels in my dreams whispered melodies that I could see
Believe
The key
Cold hearted serpents please leave
I'm still searching for me
Old, departed assurance, we weave
So I'm told it started with fervency
We bleed
A mold so guarded with working seeds
We flee
I say, not to be
Let the love which burned start
The key I speak of is to my heart
Liam Zevoughn 7/22/20

DISTRAUGHT

The word
I have faith in this
It's absurd but I remember when I shared a room with a satanist
& my dreams were void
You were right to stay toward
The medicine
We were in a psych ward with many worn skeletons
Distraught
This was me
But my heavenly thought is for you to be free
Liam Zevoughn 7/24/20

GOD

In the depths of psychopathy, I ate nothing
The memory is fuzzy
I took all this effort to create you now I just want you to love me
Dear God, a sweet prayer to thee
You always are the same
I will venture there to see
I will never again write in vain
Now I hope you will agree
Dear God, the intricacy of your workmanship
Cannot be matched
Even the bee is equipped
Every patch
Is unfathomable to I
Johnny told me that
Different is every eye
Dear God, please tell
Please dawn on me
That I won't go to Hell & I can make songs for thee
This can be
Heaven sent
As was me
Leaven these dreams
I want you to love me
Resin as to fiends as writing is to me
Liam Zevoughn 7/24/20

◦ GHOSTS

This time
I will lose in strife
There's a thin line between reality & delusion in life
Sweet intricate lies you bemuse me
I am lost
I believed I seethed from the used, see
I referred to my home as a pile of bones
I live in sin
Yet I flourish
I say, the angels at my death, where have you been?
The dull turned null & called me worthless

Funny the only thing I remember is fear
These ghosts are trying to kill me here
Liam Zevoughn 7/26/20

Northern Lights

I love when the moon is more in sight
Than the dark
I smoked those northern lights
& now a latency has gripped my heart
Wait & see the angels hark
Radiant
Like the car that hit me
I fade it
The star which pities
Don't fake me
The flesh is so itchy
I tried to be a rebel but they wanted to use & keep me
As an excuse
Caught between the devil & the deep blue sea
Just hit me, muse
My wish
Is that I knew where I was going with this
He's glowing white, see?
Our life is a blunder & I wonder what my vice will be
I shall fill this plot with love & taste
It took all of 30 minutes to fall from grace
Overflowing cup
Brittany, maybe that's just growing up
Liam Zevoughn 8/5/29

DEATH

I said it best
Be well read; I'm using these breaths to say everything we know is death
Fraying
Decaying
Everything we know will go to deteriorating
We're just waiting
This is true
I said everything is dead & soon it will be you
Itchy flesh
Woe to the show, Vicky, I know I said it best
All we know is death
Will I claim what is rightfully mine?
Or will I stay in a freak's nursery rhyme
Upon arrival of the west
I know what the best is
All we know is death & the only thing that glows will be a bioluminescence
May God heal their wrath
Do you think Hades whispered to the pale horseman to take everything in his path?
Liam Zevoughn 8/6/20

The Torture of the Souls on Earth

Hear the screams
Definite wails
Another tear would seem
Almost too much to bear
In the spirit, I scathed that old dirt
But these demons don't fear it
The torture of the souls on earth
The chastisement
The control
Of an evil so far below the surface
There's no boat to row
People, you must bar & sew
& that service
Was divine
I long for a purpose
I see that being alive will define
The odds
But may this please no other God but the true
Creator
May the dawn be ever in your favor
A day without a drawn equator
A bouquet thrown about a dusty elevator
Grey shone enough to
Find that old fellow
The one which burns as a factory radiator
I can't do this anymore
I grow even fader
I am torn
So done with a mindless dictator
Never fear the dreams
Which never fail
Hear the screams
Definite wails

I don't wish for old dirt
Hear the torture of the souls on earth
Liam Zevoughn 8/7/20

GHOST WHO HAUNTS THE STAGE

I hope the prayers burn good
Incense
I must say, I miss that old hood, but distance is best
The star's name was Wormwood
Where is all my sense?
The car's fame burned as it should
To diffuse this debacle, I'll give two sense
The star's name was Wormwood
A curious, celestial extravagance
Turn if you could
He is furious, what could you have against
Wormwood
I know His wrath is detrimental
Show, for this mask is not gentle
Below, is the past
I say, today, they need a prayer ten fold
I've come too close but I still want this page
It is immortal
I am the ghost who haunts the stage
I threw away my chance at being royal
Now confined to a cage
I want to get close to God's ways
I am the ghost who haunts the stage
Liam Zevoughn 8/14/20

Past Over

Unblemished slain lamb
Can you
Understand
The message doesn't hurt me or my veins
But I know that God's mercy reigns
Past over is the angel
I will not fall to the beast
The Passover feast is a supportive angle
Let me eat, at least
This disdain can
Outlast
Unblemished slain lamb
I will do my best to understand
Liam Zevoughn 8/14/20

DELIRIOUS

Let's break this
Little by little
Hark this
I may be in darkness but I try to speak to you in riddles
Uncanny & mysterious
We whittle
Many are delirious
With the sun I was trying to woo
Win affection
I have better things to do than hide under the tree of psychopathy
or rejection
This is true
This is gospel
I have better things to do, like the impossible
Liam Zevoughn 8/14/20

PERSONAL SYMPHONY

I had hoped royalty was watching me
This was not something I did consciously
I thought I had sewn the key
Verse & all
Personal
Symphony
They'd rather see me in the pen
Their noises
Whispered voices through the trees again
It hurts to stall
The key
Personal
Symphony
Just burn a little more
See
The more we whittle this war the more I need my symphony
Worse than all is your tee
The pitch
My personal symphony was one to remember- a stitch
& absurd is the soon
Cold-hearted
I hope I am murdered before this mold is parted
Liam Zevoughn 8/20/20

CD

I can smell the rain in the air
Won't someone please care
Please believe
The tree of psychopathy has me wrapped in its sweet symphonies
A beautiful snare
Thy culling, fair and daring revelry
Will never be clear
So dulling to care
Mulling a hare
Nulling to spare a level tee
I have nothing here but the devil can see
Habitual fears, psychopathy
Seeking hope in rafters of white light
The ugliest chapter of my life
Was that of no fight
I can't escape any branch of lunacy-it's too tight
I bet you wish you could beat me
Truancy of infectious blight
Hellish arrest
I remember the smell of that CD & I would relish in rest
Brittany & I went without sight
Liam Zevoughn 9/2/20

EUPHORIA

Sprightly white light
Euphoria
Lightly burnt spirit
Your tone, I hear it, dysphoria
Thy fine sight
Detected my line
Fight
Deflected the night
My kite
Resurrected to heights
Unbeknown
My deemed sight
Dost thy throne
Belittle?
Foster this sewn riddle

Rubber, dented in an old shed
Yearn
The government is messing with my head again
Turn
John, you're good people
Never again wrestle with this evil
Respect I send
I will paint on this easel
Liam Zevoughn 9/3/20

Au Revoir

For now I bid thee farewell
Au revoir
Respect to officer Darrell
Forgive what these eyes saw
Sing to me a spell
As if the waters tested
As if I could see
I remember when officer Darrell arrested me
Arrêté
& the tale I told he
Was divine intervention
Was something more than just being
A flatline question
Left me bruised with much feeling
Sentiment
Je te connais bien
I try to speak to you in tongues
A language of love so they tell
So raw
But now I will bid thee farewell
Au revoir
Liam Zevoughn 9/3/20

LIBERTY HALL

They ask "How are you?"
I reply
Very high
I used to be flirty after all
I remember making Mrs. Berry cry in liberty hall
& when will the least become sublime?
Faulted in brillance
But exalted for resilience
All I asked for was peace of mind
Liam Zevoughn 9/7/20

Infériorité

This prison is done
Will deteriorate
Woe to the one who sings of annihilation
I am inferior to this date
Infériorité
I may say je
Je suis
A mess but a sweet song to thee
I want to find her
A trouvé-she is burned
To those who decipher these words
I leave a trace-those scars you earned
I mourn the death of a dim light
Je pleure
I was born in place to begin right-I cannot wait to occur
Liam Zevoughn 9/12/20

Douce vérité

The erosion runs
There goes sanity
If we outlast the explosion of our sun
Here comes vanity
In the park, this a must, for tales
That feeling when only darkness prevails
Douce vérité
Enough to rot the bones in your head
Erosion
Douce vérité is not sewn in thread
Addiction, can you really defeat youth?
Douce vérité
Sweet truth
At first I had doubt but now lay dead in a booth
Cœur pur
Vrai cœur
Tell me you are sure
I scathed that old luth
But why?
Come to me sweet truth because you cannot tell a lie
I fail today
All hail douce vérité
Liam Zevoughn 9/13/20

BEDTIME

I don't care to hand you the stuff
I am your friend
I wish I could write enough to kill big hair bands again
May God grace these bloody cuffs
I say, what a place to empathize the rough

The best
Won us
The word became flesh & dwelt among us

Death I will not leave my faith in
So here's to my dear friend, Kaiden
Swellings of courage
But when the bell rings
It's bedtime for the flourished
Once Hell sings
There will be none nourished
This shell brings
Enough to push the furthest
Liam Zevoughn9/29/20

The Ghost of the Traffic Light

If I didn't stand
If more
Bloomed
If I didn't have liquor & death in my hands-
We all are doomed
Can the ones down the hall hark?
I have been stumbling in the dark
With fevers
The scars on my heart spark
I remember screaming in Steve's basement
Among friends
I scathed the skeleton enough to taste it
Curse ends
The ghost of the traffic light looms
But what's beyond another imminent doom?
Hurting is the model of fine
Taste
Defeat at all times
I'm nursing a bottle of sweet wine in my line & I will chase
Forever coming undone
Ever after
Sever my tongue & love me lavender
Liam Zevoughn 10/13/20

PLEURÉSIE

This tale I am finishing
Hope a better day will arise
But my body will keep on diminishing
I wrote this letter on the occasion of my demise
Pleurésie
I thought this would be easy
May the secret dawn
Poumons de goudron
& this ladder hasn't enough rungs
Douce mort
I try to speak to you in tongues
Who could this be for?
Douce mort
Douce mort
Douce mort
Can I defeat what is left?
Sanity is running past
Sweet death I am coming to you, again, at last
No release
Serenades of jovial finesse
I can't lie to police
So bestow hellish arrest
Poumons de goudron
Pleurésie
My sanity has gone
This wasn't easy
Liam Zevoughn 10/14/20

Apostasy Hymn

I watched her mascara run streams
Sierra
I'd like to know if you were really as broken as you seemed
Do confide
Back in the day, I say, all was a lie
Relaxing in a sway, today, we found a better way to slowly die

These days I spend pacin'
Waiting for a sign
I search for a benign line in constellations
Fading for a shine
Hurts to look behind and see people chasin'
I only ever wanted to be kind

I will again, sin
This is where I begin
This is my apostasy hymn

But don't know if I believe in filler
I will write just enough to sever
Brittany, I think I see you differently because I want to be like
that forever
I won't hang on fences
Never
I don't believe in coincidence since I found my perfect weather

Myself
Is mistaken to be
Here's to the felt
All that I love has been taken from me
This is the hand I was dealt

I mourn the death of a dim
Light

This is my apostasy hymn
Let me know what you call right
Liam Zevoughn 11/1/20

INSPIRE

I will read
I will call the rest a liar
The alcohol in me says to plant a seed but the other says to inspire
Liam Zevoughn 10/26/20

Brilliance

Your tee
Absurd
Hinge it's
Lore
I just murdered 15 minutes
Will the Lord cover all the gore?
Evanescence
These lessons bore but tell me a nothing like you did before
Convalescent
Normality
I've tried & tried to open the door to immortality
In vain
I said your tee is absurd
No shame in infinites
I said I murdered 15 minutes trying to conjure these words in
sheer brilliance
Liam Zevoughn 11/10/20

A QUESTIONABLE DEED

A benign smile
Showed me the way
& the pain in wild tempests say
Wrong defenses
Show me how
Show me now or suffer the consequences
A raindrop blessed my insides
I'm telling you this is true but obsessed am I with my own demise
Hail this cycle in our prison
Too many hood-like highs I have smothered
Aneurism
Nothing like waving goodbye to a thousand mothers if they can't
respect the wisdom
& yet wrong am I
To believe
I bet this song will ask why
A questionable deed
Liam Zevoughn 11/12/20

STRANGER

When you meet a stranger all is shrouded
Let thy be not clouded
Let your defenses be ever routed
& the consequences be doubted
When you meet a stranger I hark the sweet divinity of mystery
Tar on the feet of a burlesque angel in me
This is history
No anger in the eyes; you have earned to reach
The benefit
But when it's a stranger you meet hope that they're heaven sent
Liam Zevoughn 11/13/20

HERE

I often wonder how I got here
The rotting decay diminishes
The visions of a boy dreaming of fear finishes with a tear
Wishes
I've forgotten under the sheer
Pressure
I often wonder how I got here
I used all my best tests to uphold for the lesser
Rotten lumber is dear
To the fire
I often wonder how I got here
Let my urn burn as destiny to inspire
When I was younger I was a deer
In the headlights of a sultry death wish
I often wonder how I got here
& ignorance can be bliss
Liam Zevoughn 11/13/20

Recession

Who could those cuffs be for?
A ferocious question
Lord knows I fall before the ultimate lesson
The more I grow
The farther I sew my confession
Jesus Christ is Lord & that's all I know
May this question never be in recession
Liam Zevoughn 11/13/20

THE LIST

Upon a burning helium I wish
The inevitability
Dawned is learning, this is the list, if it doesn't finish than kill me
I wish for groundbreaking candle wicks
Burning infernally
I wish for sound making, cataclysmic gifts
Discerning eternally
I wish for
A microcosm
That I could write into existence
Flowers are pretty before they blossom but who would miss this?
I am psychotic so pill me
I am another
Sweet, melodic pains fill me
I will say hello to my brother
But wave goodbye to silly
I wish for lavender
A calmness unseen
I wish I could have her but she is willing to deceive
I miss the kiss
Which set me free
I just have to be Liam
This is the list
Upon a burning helium I wish
I pray that God feels them
Maybe a call from Genesis
What a state to be in
It's you I miss
God, forgive this vile sin
I can't stop with this
Where do I begin?
Liam Zevoughn 11/13/20

DEAR FUTURE SELF

Dear future self,
Today, I am 22 years old
Here is the lost & found shelf
I say, I may do
The impossible
& continue spreading the gospel
To the best of my ability
I will discern hospital files & know what is real to me
Questions I have earned
Paracetamol effects
Two important lessons I have learned
Are patience & respect
Immortality, I knock on your door
In a cold prison
Those four words of wisdom are Jesus Christ is Lord
Hail the only risen
The void, the hole
Affecting brothers
I'm always paranoid but the goal was a grasp on respecting others
Seeds I have planted
Inevitable decision
I never take a day for granted
My pencil is full of words of precision
Making sure the angel of death is not, again, on my shoulder
Not so, this is odd
The greatest thing about getting older is growing closer to God
May God bless this hymn
No more sin
I am feeling my best when I am wearing a grin on my face again
Curse my faulty wiring
Few find the way
I'm saying I live true to myself by inspiring to people every day
Liam Zevoughn 11/13/20

THE EPISODE

I'll never forget the days
My own mind bemused me
Never forget the praise of God, who cannot lie or lose me

In this period of time I cried
I confessed
Here is the obsessed

People met me by the river stream
Raising the question
Can you lessen or was this really a dream?
You wouldn't take my confession because I was a fiend

I am unworthy
True
She said she loved me but I said please, don't hurt me
Now I think I love you too
Liam Zevoughn 11/13/20

Surreptitious

Sounding out the vowel
Under the tree of psychopathy
Round & round the down
Round about to see
Expecting the sun
Passing the key
Thou has become
Ill to me
Tracing my lips
I will not tell
Of secrets of the dead
Understand this spell
So indescribable in my head
Liam Zevoughn 11/13/20

Virtuous Boy

There was once a boy virtuous
Who screamed to hurt is to rust
Who shew the brightest lore
A hue never seen before
Unfitted & transgressive he lived in dust
Liam Zevoughn 11/13/20

CARICATURES

I rust in the dark
I bleed among the lost hearts
That were lining up

To greet vague caricatures
I hope to defeat the sure
Liam Zevoughn 11/13/20

Appetency

I was unfortunate enough to be the absentee
Striving for excellence
Appetency
A convalescence once strived for only wellness
Tapping to see what's hollow
Wouldn't you agree?
I am rapping just to smite the stigma, won't you follow?
The sap from the pine tree
Will not suppress me here
Appetency, you are ambitious, you are near
You breathe for me & I control the fear
I see only obscurity
My appetency is for purity
Liam Zevoughn 11/13/20

BRAVE

At times I wonder
At times I relive
I pulled the pieces asunder
Now an ode I will give
I will create my own ride
Evil people
I will start the great divide
A sweet upheaval in the way we all commit suicide
May the righteous die with finesse
May the rest find their way
I tested
I prayed
A convalescent I will remain
But at times I wonder
Even ponder the jinn
Is my everything a blunder? What trouble could I be in?
Will I ever receive revelation
May these words haunt the grave
Condensation on the window says to be brave
Liam Zevoughn 11/13/20

Avaunt

Avaunt
Flee
Before it's you I haunt & not the weary
You could say I am a phantom
Say with ease
Gray-blue & some
Antifreeze

On their bikes, in two, they did taunt
I wondered who was there to plant them
Avaunt, avaunt, avaunt
I am a phantom

Was this necessary to the feeble mind
No one knows
Love may vary, just be kind
Throw your stones

Get away; avaunt
Gauntly form
All I wanted used to be to conform
Liam Zevoughn 11/13/20

Heroine

Hail the plant walking without feet
It's been my heroine
After awhile I thought I'd try to write a concrete poem
The blood
The cure to my skeleton
Was this flood of archaic medicine
The lines & space
I never dropped my pencil in the waste
I'm sure
I never dropped my full defense until this phase
I hope to stay pure
My notebook withers
Goodbye, my friend
No looks will prosper hither, I will make amends
I'm all in but tend to fall
Tell Dalton, my friend, death is coming for us all
Writing has liberated me & my expressions
All alone
I said my body has faded but I need to answer some questions of old
Of immortality
& making the first move is just formality
Observing tradition?
Spare me fairly & join me on my expedition
If I could write a concrete poem
I would first say believe
All my life I've shew a persona which is naïve
I fail
I can't defeat
Hail the plant walking without feet
Liam Zevoughn 11/14/20

LIGHT OF LIME

Refrain
From the luth
Obsessed & confessed
I hope you use your savior's name in truth
This was less than a test
But more of an awakening
The reeling I'm feeling more than fake beings
Soothe
Jesus is the name
Bleeding ulcers; I'm trying to say in this culture we should refrain
from the vain
I will see them
Again
I constantly think this is my last few minutes of freedom
I don't comprehend
These days I notice the phases of the moon
Waiting for a sign
I have spent time in full bloom but I wonder when I will see the
light of lime
Liam Zevoughn 11/17/20

WORN

Let me think
Ponder a nirvana
The null seem to sink but I had Jesus speak to me while high
on marijuana
& the vision
That rendered me conscious
Related to my constant Indecision
May he have grace on us
Many brave but few who coo risen
Never alone sail in the depths of agnosticism
I'll never be enough to feel
The sweetest gifts are of love & free will
& despite war
I breathe
The last time I kissed a women was in a psych ward but I still believe
I could never be a guaranteed savior
Blessings in swarms
God I do seek your unmerited favor
I am just a little worn
Liam Zevoughn 12/1/20

DIVINE DEALING

I'm just trying to be
Don't get no clearer
I know you look something like me, God, that's why I'm talking
in the mirror
Pleading
Got my mind playing tricks I hope to fix my internal bleeding
Inside, a wooden crucifix, a kiss for the nocturnal heeding
Tides
To the surface ticks & beating
No lies
I am transfixed with healing
Spies
I must say, my attitude flew past the grace but faced a divine dealing
Liam Zevoughn 12/2/20

INTENTIONS

I always want true
Intentions
You must leave before I haunt you
But the realest I won't even mention
Divinity
Sweet lavender
You are so ill to me but I have to rapture
Up & out of the mold
Forever turning
They are corrupt but doubt they are cold
Never discerning
Praising the God who cannot forsake me
These lulls turn full
I am constantly wondering if this is the moment God will take me
Dull is my pencil
Hell is hot
Carted cigarettes
Since I started expressing myself I don't know how to stop
Hello death-
Liam Zevoughn 12/5/20

LETTER TO MOTHER NATURE

Mighty in essence
May God sustain the
Other pure
This convalescent still affects the best but I admire Mother Nature
I remember being in your garden
& ceasing the rebellion
Farther than creasing
We sing well in
Our broken skeleton
Well I just need to say
I will not be grey or fade & today I have found my medicine so
now I pray that I can stay in the grace & place of ardent lessons
This quill
Will kill
Dependency
Forget the sheer thrill of a free will but just stand still and I will
defend your tee
I recall your morbid fascination
The one I once called friend
Passed me by without inflation & left me to no end
So I won't be dismal
Or dreary
Dull is my pencil
The weary bloomed in full
Entirely null
Inspire me
Murderous voices may tell me to cull
You must quiet me
Forever I shall paint on this paper
Let it be
This is my letter to Mother Nature; please heed
Liam Zevoughn 12/6/20

A QUESTION TO GOD

Here burns the cue
Surrender me
All hail truth
Please remember me
This is an odd lesson, no lies
I am still burning & turning; but if I could ask God a question
It would be why
Why did I have to die to discover your virtue?
Heroic declaration
High due to the most gracious weed of truth
Poetic, fair desperation
You
Never left me but I suffered inflation
True
You, forever sighing, took on my question with design & I was
left finding
The line
Peace
Never confining but always sublime
Crease
Severing, grinding
Release
It seems I may never circumvent this cancer
Confessin'
I love you Lord & I think I have the answer to this question
Liam Zevoughn 12/7/20

Eulogy

He was elegant
Puzzled
He can't come back now
We shall stay muzzled at the way he lived
He done flew south
He was so bright but there's no right to keep his name in our mouth
& was he given enlightenment?
Shrouded
All his time amounted to
An oddity
& the legacy is fog to me
Sure he took a strange route
But he is okay now
He never had to fight & was so bright but we have no right to keep
his name in our mouth
You & me
Are done
This is my self written eulogy
I now watch all of you under the sun
Liam Zevoughn 12/7/20

NULL

I want to erase
Define
I want all to know about God's grace & perfect light of lime
Here I will savor
Earned paper
I want all to know about God's unmerited favor
Birds & all creation
Were once whole
Personal
Separation
These are the null
Defying the rest
Forgive me, I am lost
I was trying my best to show God that I would die on the cross
With him
An ember & my head shattered
Exult
Remember when I said no matter what I say it's not your fault?
Not your fault
To just surrender to the red
I must say, at her, I love you after all
Remember when I said no matter what I say it's not your fault?
Liam Zevoughn 12/11/20

DISTRACTION

& my bones fisted
But had I always known Christ existed?
I knew too the panic in your eyes but as it seemed was a dream; I
didn't think I was wicked but was soothed by lullabies

Calling me a liar
Somehow will not suffice
Let these words inspire, Jesus Christ knows, this is fire, fire, fire
I called & he answered
I have fallen on an absurd
Angle
Let me breathe before you leave and then, my sanity, I will strangle
Why doesn't anybody stop me
Taint the pure
Every tree I paint is a tree of psychopathy & I am sure
My heart is dark & muddy
What can I say?
I love when Kid Cudi tells me it'll be okay
I'm feeling, I'm passin'
I am one hardcore distraction
May these words be everlastin'
Liam Zevoughn 12/17/20

CLOUD OF RESURRECTION

I once yearned for affection
I once burned
My cloud of resurrection
Turned me
To full bloom
Room, I confess, is attuned
But the moons
The way they fume
Has got me wanting to come home soon
This section is for the lame
I said I once yearned for affection but now know that it is vain
Nothing to gain
No direction
Woe to the witch who cries anemic lullabies
My cloud of resurrection was a stitch for all the lies
Pardon this thread & forget your foes
Detection
My cloud of resurrection started at my head until it reached my toes
No need for deflection
It sewed
So to Jesus Christ, who spoke this cloud into existence
Thank you
My life awoke in this
Bloom
I am already ready to go but is this faux?
The cloud entombed
Now I yearn
For the celestial rooms
For extraterrestrial vacuums
For extra sea
This is true urgency
Send love to the truly tuned
Don't know if they want you or me
Will you take or give?

Tension grew
Though my resurrection was short lived
I now only trust few
& may this scream perfection
To the loons
I know that I am one of you but I can't shake my moment of
resurrection
My mic drops with a boom
Liam Zevoughn 12/21/20

Twilight Shines

I will wave goodbye to past
Twilight shines
The biggest highlight of my life is making people laugh
That is mine
I will praise the Sun Setter
"Go get her."
Do I have enough love for the words of Jesus in red letters?
We see the rough & absurd
Threaders
Obsessors
A convalescent's big time header
"The wounded have the upper hand."
Whispered in my ear by better understanding
Sand
To this I will cling & I wish there was a landing
A fine white line
Night
Signs
Twilight shines, twilight shines, twilight shines
Will there ever be a home for this broken skeleton?
White light in rafters of peace
Lord knows laughter is the best medicine but it is hard to cease
Liam Zevoughn 1/4/20

Haunted Coast

When it's His will
The risen quill
The devil tries to blind me with visions still
My family in a hearse
I was left alone
To suffer
Insane is this verse but this works
I do love her

This life is rougher
This will lose its luster
How much tracing grace could you muster?
The pits are worse
My family in a hearse
Did God send me here to suffer a lonesome curse?

Alleviate this flame
Heaven-sent are you
What a B-rate game because I only ever wanted to be true
Hello unwanted ghost
You are history
Sew my haunted coast & leave the place a mystery
Liam Zevoughn 1/5/20

LIBRARY OF MY MIND

The voices I heard
Inspired
Something about being surrounded by words
Has me wanting to start a fire

The library of my mind
Is vast
The very thought of God's signs in the past
Has got me wanting to come home fast

Death I shan't fear
Truthfully, I am obsessed
This mess
Is sad
I remember taking tequila shots with Jess & dad

But results may vary
God's signs; sometimes scary
Stand in my line
Welcome to the library of my mind
Liam Zevoughn 1/6/21

AGAIN

I just found this pen
If I could only coax the forgiving
I am the ghost who haunts the living
Hardly a test
I am an artery, I do confess

Wanting to be true
I've been everywhere & dared but I'm still not done haunting you

What is beyond but out of confusion?
So I just found this pen
I keep winning when I plan on losin'
Here's to hoping Jesus Christ finds me again

I can't forget transgressions that haunt even me
Respect
I don't think anybody could want me or my side affects
Liam Zevoughn 1/8/21

PORCELAIN

Of course you are in
Sticks & tin won't break my skin
I am made of porcelain
Of all my inability still people admire
I am branded with hostility & was purified with fire
I will assert; this is true
I am the lame
Why do I comfort you? Our flaws are not the same
My smile is fake
See?
I've been sublime but not fine, won't someone break me?
Liam Zevoughn 1/6/21

Freak Scientist

Your wings have scars
I sing of delirious Tzars
I want to show you how but now you put me in a jar
Now I'm sure I exist
Affect
You are a freak scientist & I am the subject
This brings me too far
Your wings have scars-what does it mean?
I turned full in fentanyl clots
Your experimental dreams
Must stop
A burning star
Missed me
I am in a jar so the angels can't kiss me
No bliss
No texts
You are a freak scientist & I am the subject
Ring around the star
Quickening
Your wings have scars & it is sickening
This affects
My liberty
Freak scientist-subject
Why must you bring me misery?
Liam Zevoughn 1/7/21

Survive It All

During everything we fuss
We make commotion
But I am telling you about Jesus
& the sweet ocean
Will I pretend
Or live?

It is amazing there is no sin he can't forgive
A hue I could not believe
Hail truth
I will sail to the booth
& never again need

Pencil shavings on my desk
It is indescribable
Here's to the rest; now let's survive it all
Liam Zevoughn 1/7/21

I Want To Feel Alive

Yes, I am high
I kept believing
Yes, I am tarnished
I never wonder why the youth are unvarnished

I want to die
She crept, relieving
I want to feel alive
The fruit of life I am peeling

I never wonder why
The elephant is adorned
No, I'm not harsh
I'm just shy & torn, of course

I will give you immortality
You will not indulge in this tree
I will give you another God to follow so it doesn't have to be me

You were only waiting, patiently
For the love of choice
God, you are truly poetic
We were only fading, innately
Gave us dominion over wit

Poetic

Into the vibe
I do exist
Underneath tides
It's not hard to miss

There's lies a new world
The most eternal atmosphere
There is a curl I savor here
Could this be my career?

Holy Ghost
You are inspiring
I wish to be there most; I would get some new wiring

Truth stung my lips when I spoke of you
The youth sunk their ships but I awoke with truth
Liam Zevoughn 12/12/19

DUST

Will these words be famous?
He spoke in dust
Today, I've been looking for a way to spontaneously combust
I thought I heard a woman scream
From the grapevine
I thought I had a little dream but then the devil took my
Machine

Vain is us
We must
I've been looking to spontaneously combust
Shots straight to the liver
I meet fate
No more cuts; I feel no shivers

Never in cuffs
No lust
I want to spontaneously combust

I don't want to rust so I will
Spontaneously combust
Liam Zevoughn 1/8/21

I'm Sorry

Don't you thrill me
Lie to me
My God, why won't you kill me

The well is full
Of my tears
Now I will be dismal
Fearful, dreary
I am abysmal
You will never fear me

I didn't think the cave would cave in
But it did
I remember looking at you & thinking "am I attracted?"

Be well read
Apostasy
Maybe I listen to music because I can't accept the fact I'm not dead
A kiss to the rotten sea

It is draining to be optimistic
When you're dreams are on the pavement twisted
I will shed another tear to discern the night; starry
I am rusty but Dusty, I'm sorry, I'm sorry, I'm sorry
Liam Zevoughn 1/8/21

FREE

I can never only be
May God forgive this sin & score
Now I am feeling free
As free as never before

I will ponder a nirvana
A vice arrested me
Transfixed with marijuana
I will free my mind but that girl tested me

Thought my spoken words were bad?
I hone it, open absurdity
The moment I became free I slurred my speech
Leave the pot to lure me

This sin's score
Is finished
This is the moment I became free as never before so let
authority diminish
Liam Zevoughn 1/9/21

Rainbow Eyelashes

I have so much respect for what He gave
It hurts
I got one foot in the grave
One foot in church
Breathing does sound easy
Can't open I'm broken
Will death ever appease me?

May the planets align
& remember my name
Nursing a bottle of sweet wine in my line
& what of fame?

To fight is vain so go
Can't tell if he meshes or clashes
I saw every color of the rainbow within my eyelashes
Liam Zevoughn 1/9/21

I Want to be With God

I write with a grin
I scrabbled my chin
I've dabbled in sin trying to begin-it's pretty odd
I fight but rarely win-It's time for me to be with God

So
No fuss
In Mexico-I'll be on that bus

An event soon to unfold
It is pretty odd
This is better than all the gold, story untold, I want to be with God
Liam Zevoughn 1/10/21

YESTERDAY'S SUN

&
If tomorrow comes
We willingly borrow a sun from yesterday
If it is done
You'll be spilling me & letting me run, fester & pray
Will I become
A product of the years of pestered rays?
An odd duct of a peer's lettered phase?
We're out of luck, here's to hopeful better days
I can't even breathe
But Gerard
Are we far? Can you give a reason to believe?
Shrouded
Enchantment runs
This time together amounted to blacker lungs
This mind had better stack some rungs
Bliss finds severed, distanced sons
Feelingly, sorrow comes
What to say?
We willingly borrow a sun from yesterday
Liam Zevoughn 1/10/21

PERSEVERE

I need, yet I breathe
Yet I flourish
Yet I unlocked the secrets of the trees & their purpose

O, star
I feel your heat, so fold me
With every sigh I think about the lie you told me
My heart will speak
Will defeat
I have a due date
What I seek will deteriorate
This week I feel inferior
Fate
I shan't fear
Lord knows the sewn will grow here
Seek
Reap
Who sees that I've unlocked the secrets of the trees?
The weak will weep

We have but little score
But persevere
If there is to be another civil war
There will be hell to fear
Liam Zevoughn 1/11/21

I Missed It

All I wanted to do was grow up rappin'
With the sun I was trying to woo
You know when you wait all your life for something to happen-
I will lose at exactly this move

Stoic
Raw sense
I will be your poet & you will be my audience
I will serve it
Perspective
I am not your poet because you deserve it I just respect & forgive

What earns history's breeze
But a harmless defeat?
When I'm at terms with a mystery I feel at peace; this is surely sweet

The light of the streetlamp
Bemuses me
The might of her sweet stamp confuses me
The likes of a pure deceitful amp
Loses me
White light is a sure defeat for the damp
This amuses me
& foolishly
I wave
But the rules are in me so tonight I fall back in the grave
Every fool can see that I might cave
No jewelry will be saved
The music is dooming me & I crave
Only yearning
But fusing me is the brave
Never burning
Losing she-
Now I will fade

Now I will fall back in the grave
Coming out of the shadows
Is your ghost
Invading
With the tube serenading I will say that I am suffocating
Berating
Enough fading
My mind & your line are consolidating
At the mercy of this pen I am greying
Glimmering, beaming, raying
While shivering, screaming & fraying
I will write & reach the top
Can I ever be known as smart?
When will you stop? Long live my car crash heart

The light of the streetlamp
Bemuses me, far, to the key
I am constantly wondering: is this the mark of my enemy?
Lacking can & is
Absence of color
A beautiful black canvas
Could someone lend some defense for my brother?
I just wanted to be rappin'
The grave; I will rinse it
I waited all my life for something to happen & I missed it
Liam Zevoughn 1/15/21

CABIN IN THE WOODS

I am left here to inspire-
Astound
It is winter & crunching snow is the only sound
I am in a cabin, all alone
I find the strength to smile
The next neighbor isn't for miles-no phone

Hot peppermint tea
Shall stain my insides
I will rot
Heaven-sent
Finally free
I hail the ominous light
The sun
My only stronghold
Dances on the snow
When this begun, I know, I told
& now I will sew

Vanity
I confess
Vain
My family will attest-I'm insane
Please excuse my frozen vessels & veins
Be at ease
Lose
I open a paper crane
Why is there so many rules
To the likes of the same
Fools?
Why is there so much to do?
I will let the walls ooze
I will fuse
I will leave this here to woo

To be used

I do remember cold September rains
& death's sweet motion
Please excuse
My frozen veins
But I admire the frozen ocean
Around thee
& the one that surrounds me

Its so cold-I'm grabbin' at my hoods
I struggle with the life I found
I'll never forget the cabin in the woods-I'm left here to astound
Liam Zevoughn 1/22/21

Painted Hands

Anxious
But my mind can see
If I truly am art's savior I bet they still want to crucify me

At the mercy of this pen, I weep
He spoke in dust
I am starlight & wine
On that road to Damascus I was blind
Wondering what's true
Under my lore is my core but Lord, who are you?

A fainted man
Will diminish
My painted hands will finish
& tell a lore
& will leave the moral in it just as poets did before
I waited on fans
Years
But my painted hands will speak here without fear so kindly hold
your tears
Faded dams will conspire
These
Painted hands
Will start a fire

A weakling
So frail
Will cease
I will wave goodbye to failed peace & the sprinkling priest
Whom I love most
Always close are you so thank you ghost

Sew me
I am

A machine
Still odd but try not to put the god of tobacco & nicotine
First
I will fade her
So here's to the true creator
Who will quench my thirst
I broke long ago
But try not to make it worse
So, to my foes
I will embellish a hypnotic tree
Decorative patterns
Finally free on paper & here I savor the tee-all that matters
My best could not confess
To the raw ugliness
I would not wish tobacco on my worst foe
I attest
I need a key to the tee that will release me
As far as it goes

They battle with rage
This feud excused all mood
It rattled my cage-I'm asking what's the deal with people being rude
Contemplating on why man fell
Cleanse with sage
Constantly, this week, I seek Emmanuel
Paddle in the page
This
Rattled
My cage
I thought I had sewn the key
I amounted to dust
Thanks for only talking to me when you disagree
This is a must
Let us praise God, that bell rung
I was born to say "I came & sung."
I mourn the day I let a piece of hell into my lungs

God bless
Tainted cans of blue
The odd will confess that these painted hands will haunt you

Seeking to woo you with metaphorical lessons
I'm confessin to the past & I only ask rhetorical questions
Sometimes I can spell
I have too much heart in the dark; I seek Emmanuel

What was this about? You think I still want you?
Consecrated to the ardent thought I shout
These painted hands will haunt you
Liam Zevoughn 1/22/21

BURNING BUSH

Never forget the ruins
Will tell
I hold on to who I once was because time is an illusion
We are not in Hell
No color is when it hardest
To breathe
Long live the Lord's heaven sent artists & death to my broth-
er's disease

Sometimes I get angry with myself because I had faith in death
The light of lime
Surely withers
Running out of breath
The ghost-the shivers
I will look behind to see
If it's true
If you doubt God's credibility
It will not end well for you
Smoking
Behind their backs
Was dirty
The Bible is full of scientific facts
He is worthy
Beaming, raying
Will please us
The grave be fine & sane
I'm praying for Jesus to save me from every kind of pain

The poets
This rap missed them
I have not foes so here goes another sewing baptism
Without a doubt I tell you it hurts to feel
It's upsetting but I'm never forgetting the serpent that struck my heel
May this pen fold

Profound
I begun with a sun & some green emerald clouds
Forgive the sins committed while I was out of consciousness
I was broken
Honest
Long live the bad, bruised fox
Dear dad
Thank you for not taking away my music box

Lord, leaven these dreams
I am
A Machine
Jesus Christ spoke to me & showed me a vision when I was 19
I'm out of luck, stuck in this barren chamber
My best work, high on a shelf
Looking for something fair in blind anger
I can't stop since I started expressing myself
God bless the fish
Flipping about
My only wish is that I knew what mom was trippin' about
Let us not dwell on autumn's pin
Circling about is the horrific djinn
I erased every bottle of gin
Where do I begin? I said I've tasted so much sin that me & my
kin have separating skin

The envelope I wish push
I am learning the doctors swindled me
God appeared in that burning bush
& it was not a spindle tree

These letters bore
Down to my deserted core
I need some glue to do something absurd like before-my aorta
lying on the floor
Control
Inflation

No time for soul, this is manipulation
Crooks are rooking me again
Past
I must defend but I'm looking at you through the looking glass
now & then
Sometimes absurd hurts
Night to day; I'm looking for a better way to murder this verse
What to say?
Shrouded
My sunshine lays in soil bays
But today my entire mind is clouded
Just go to the acute angle
Find the muse
No abuse-this was whispered to me by an angel
Sometimes null & invalid, a wuss
But discerning so I push
God appeared
In a
Burning bush
Liam Zevoughn 1/25/21

STARSTRUCK

The water soothes
But that fire licks
What am I trying to do? I'm spending all my time trying to
use acrylics
I'm asking why is there such
Respect for sin
He spoke in swirls; I'm getting lost in a world who still rejects him
Will my fate unfurl?
Will I sing this hymn?
Nowadays I'm in a hazy phase but still love a whirlwind
Enough of the same
Mentality
Know his name?
His fame?
I have snuffed the flame of reality
Galan, no time for games
People still laugh at me
Call me sane?
But sitting in rockers are doctors who know that I'm vain
& out of my lane
I am batty
Tossed by a toy crane but I bet the coroner still wants to tag me
Dear maddy,
You are beautiful but I bet they still want to flag me
Irrational & ratty
I seethe from the lame
Sickness had me
See
Tension in the game never gained
Made y'all look faddy
I will make a fuss
But not cuss
Sitting on the shaggy
Is your lore

I need a key please agree to the madness of before
Never again will I dip my feet into waters of gore
So upsetting but not forgetting my brain sore
Never letting the evil into my core
Fretting on the most peaceful, gracious shore
Enough
The cuffs
Who could they be for?
Let's see, please agree, the score
Rowing & owning the oar
Let the birds sing & soar
These lessons bore
No questions? No I want to know more

To pass time I'm beating out a song
I find myself eating so I don't do anything else wrong
Expressing
Confessing on paper
On God's front lawn I shall savor
Finessing a painted fawn
What is death's true flavor?
Cutting & rutting the facial hair with a razor
Warning: will not suffice
This morning I find a hell raiser among mice; I shall roll the dice
Hit but don't even trip
Could you ever be nice or considerate?

I am ensnared with your words
Entangled
Is this fair? I'm getting lost in star spangled birds
They wrangle
But you're a beautiful verse
Finesse-it hurts
Searching for galaxies in the universe
This is best
I drain
Obsessed-an idea stained my brain

The epiphany caresses
Lest I am starstruck
Strained release
Nevertheless I stress I am a tool that is stuck
After 10 years of acting a fool & running amuck I think I found peace
Out of luck
Disaster here
But none to fear
I constantly want to roll the dice but not suffice I sear
I constantly haunt the soul which fights
Drear

Kyrsten this way is best
I guess
You tipped me
Today I'm looking for a better way to say how mental illness gripped me
Liam Zevoughn 2/6/21

THE LAND OF A HIGHER FREQUENCY

I can't fathom or understand
The freaks can see
The land of a higher frequency
The grim reaper, my only friend
Stood above me & left me to a fever
To no end
& leaves gathered upon my cold bed frame
Suffocating
These are rather fond of my old head pain
A lust so invading-I am suffocating
I will burn the upper-hand
Frequently, just to see
The land of a higher frequency
I have not earned a band
But by elegance In its place I have mercy in Gods grace & I will stand
In reverence
Will I go?
Will I ever know a day of severance
God willing, I will not
& that kite soared
With a string
I will never forget what was on the white board
While we sing
Glory to the Lamb & suspicion to their angel wings
This story commands positions to dangle in the form of obscurity
I wish the sands would defend the angle in which they lay
Maybe rinse me to purity
But never
Will you wrangle
With my virtue or hurt me
With judgmental words that can never be worthy
With hugs made of hurry
You are just too earthly
The freaks can see

This is absurd
For the land of a higher frequency I will be murdered
Liam Zevoughn 8/31/20

DEAD FAIRIES

Dust in my eyes
Flipping
Barely alive
Tripping over dead fairies after five

Give me reason to
Embark
I saw a black winged demon on a roof in the park

So sick of waiting
After all this time
Disaster in the mind I am hallucinating of dreams of sublime

Absurd; ever seen
I hope I never speak the wrong word
Give love to the songbird in the evergreen

He spoke in dust with sound
He said it fairly
I'm seeing what looks like dead fairies on the ground
May it never again be scary
Liam Zevoughn 6/6/21

Sigh

I'll sigh
& be absurd
I need lye but let's crucify that blackbird

I'll sigh
& notice the life of moss
This is real so tell me how it feels to be defeated by a cross

I'll sigh
With breath of profound dust
& wave goodbye to the sound of fuss

I'll sigh
I will shepherd the herd
No more fight because I'll be a bird

I will sigh & darn a new creation
Never to satisfy
Never to cry in this sweet elation
Liam Zevoughn 6/11/21

PERFECTED

May this be perfected
Spiritual grass was counted last but I see no hope if Christ is not
resurrected
But may God bless Paul
He used to be Saul
Dear God, I leave a call, don't let me fall i am too small so God,
could you leave some writing on my wall?

No defense
Too dense
The anxiety in me shall be relentless but the calm
A song
I shall speak it into existence

My last right
Is to write
Call me a master of insight but God will punish me for a past life

The world sure shines
I am well, never want to go back to Hell but I'm seeing
squirrel spines
On the ground
The aroma of viable parchment
Fills me whole
The pliable
Undeniable
Bent soul
Maniacal
Is the death roll but this is dissected
I have dulled but see no hope if Christ is not resurrected
My spinal will cave
The aroma of sweet vinyl dawned; this I will save
& the null
Will they answer us?

I am so cold but full of the cancerous

& the rules bent all
We were lost
This old luth speaks truth & I turned full in fentanyl clots

No respect for rude deflections
I weep with this pen
Resurrect me with true intentions
No time for sin
No time to think of this
A sign will do this time
In line & I will hear Incubus
That will be fine

I have written the bomb
May this be a steeple to see
Hidden in this song are people who talk about me

My appetite for malice has hardened
Once upon a time I grew in a palace
In a sunlit garden

Some things are pollution to my soul
Like evil
Command
The only solution is to love people-this is how I began

The realest ever spawned
Did not fade
But inspired
Holding on by only God's grace; I will not stay wired
No hints detected
In this note, fraying, I'm saying I see no hope if Christ is not
resurrected

On the cue I am rusty

The night is starry
So tell Dusty I must be sorry
Forever blue
Lullabies are distant
Will I ever have a clue or instance
Where
I can breathe?
Pull my lever, I do exist
This song I will leave
Liam Zevoughn 4/13/21

Lie

Screaming in another room
Is the sound of murder in tune

Dreaming of the fume
I hear
The drear
Seeming to tell of imminent doom
It's easy
Please appease me
I feel this disease is soon

I hear vices
I was heard in the pain
I feel I'll never recover from this burden nor suffer, again, in vain
The key
Please agree
Summer brought you to me again
This is me
Let it be
I wonder why you condescend

Forever I will be drawn to morbid fascination
Let me by
The led we pushed into God's creation killed every lie
Liam Zevoughn 7/4/21

Clutch

Honest
Free
Woe to know I have gone against my conscious just to see

Sometimes I text & go
I am sick
I wish I went with Rick to Mexico
But the clock ticks, so

Learn from the best
We breath the fever
Were you possessed by the angel of death or the Grim reaper
When you murdered this keeper?
When your absurd tee left me to my device's mercy
Did you think I was less or cheaper
Than a fiend?
Zest, it seems, left the freezer
Now, this is a dream
No beeper
I can't even see her
Enough? Please deem
I will hear Seether
Forget the obscene
She bought the creamer but honestly gleamed
An angelic fragrance
Of estrogen
Is it okay to move the
Pen
I'm stressing for a blessing for Cuba now & then
They are graving the free
As if to think a man driving a speed boat is saving me
May this mourning pen fold
Profound
I say, the score for this boring old town

Is a pleasant sound
But I'll never see her
Never be
Ever deter
My creed
Never confines but always sublime, you must see

The gift
Still in me
Sifting through the will that causes my inabilities
May you deem & dream

You must chisel away at the artist in yourself
Clutch
I rust but sizzle & fray with a harness
I'm on the shelf-this is too much
Liam Zevoughn 7/19/21

CPSIA information can be obtained
at www.ICGtesting.com
Printed in the USA
LVHW012116130921
697730LV00013B/1323

9 781662 826238